Witchcraft

Witchcraft

by Charles Alva Hoyt

Second Edition

Southern Illinois
University Press
Carbondale and Edwardsville

Library of Congress Cataloging-in-Publication Data

Hoyt, Charles Alva.
    Witchcraft / by Charles Alva Hoyt. — 2nd ed.
    p. cm.
    Bibliography: p.
    Includes index.
    ISBN 0-8093-1544-0
    1. Witchcraft.   I. Title.
BF 1566.H67   1989
133.4'3 — dc19   89-5987
                                                           CIP

The paper used in this publication meets the minimum requirements of
American National Standard for Information Sciences
— Permanence of Paper for Printed Library Materials, ANSI Z39.48-1984. ⊗

This book is dedicated to two men;

first, the late George Conklin, 1913-1963,

an outstanding witchcraft scholar and

my mentor in the field at Wesleyan;

and second, to that scholar and teacher

who paid my graduate school bills,

and was the first to introduce me to

my witch-ancestor Goody Martin,

my father, Carlyle Goodrich Hoyt.

Contents

Preface

In witchcraft studies, as in other areas of scholarly investigation, the questions are sometimes more important than the answers. This book is intended as a guide, a text, to help students, either those formally enrolled in a course, or those who have approached this fascinating subject on their own, find the way to the right questions, through an enormous mass of complex, contradictory and emotionally-charged material. "Witch" has been, and in some places still is, a term of opprobrium reserved for the most contemptible of the human race; on the other hand in our own time it often identifies a member of a small group of enlightened nature-worshipers who practice nudism, vegetarianism, and the dance. What is the relationship of these concepts to each other? Were the victims of the sixteenth and seventeenth-century mass executions members of harmless eccentric cults? Were they members of anything at all: was there in fact at any time prior to the twentieth century any truly organized body of witches? These central questions, with many other peripheral ones, are being debated today.

The problem will not be in finding answers, but in judging between them. In my opening chapter I distinguish between no less than seven schools of witchcraft belief. Each of these schools has its answers ready, and the student will find them totally irreconcilable. What this book hopes to do, is first to present these arguments in summary, with such comments as my own and other recent studies make pertinent, and then to direct the student to the sources for these arguments, the data upon which they are founded, so that after further reading he may judge between them on his own. This book then does not pretend to be an exhaustive treatment of any aspect of this area, but a guide which if used conscientiously will take the student into any such area, as deeply as he wishes to go.

Because witchcraft, like music, say, is both a discipline and a story, this book will not be confined to a single approach to its subject. Witchcraft is an historical phenomenon, with origins in the earliest periods of human culture, and succeeding developments in Babylon, Jerusalem, Athens, and Rome, as well as mediaeval and Renaissance Europe, not to mention ancient and modern Asia, Africa, and the Americas. Witchcraft is also a craft indeed, a body of knowledge which may be investigated independent of its origins. It is also a body of literature, which may be discussed as literature, or in terms of its philosphy. Rather than attempt to confine this enormous body to the procrustean bed, then, this book takes witchcraft as it presents itself; as history, as science, as literature; and, no less profitably, as occasion for furious and long-continued debate.

Those who have assisted me in this study are too numerous to be named *in toto*, but I do want to single out three for their special efforts: first, Joan E. Missall, Assistant Librarian at the Mid-Orange Correctional Facility, formerly Reference Librarian at Bennett College, for her invaluable aid in locating and securing texts for me; and then Mrs. Barbara Brenner of the Marist College Library, for her kind and continuing help; and finally my wife Mariana Schackne Hoyt, not only for her loyal assistance in the chores of copy editing, proofing, and typing, but also for her scholarly aid in the French material.

Millbrook, N.Y.   *Charles Alva Hoyt*
August 14, 1980

1. Introduction to Witchcraft

Not so long ago (the book in which he reported his experiences was published in 1966), an Englishman named James H. Neal was serving as Chief Investigations Officer in Accra, Ghana. It was reported to him that large quantities of cement, steel rods, machinery and other materials were being stolen from the Tema Port Project, and so he went down to investigate. In the course of this operation, a strange thing happened to him.

He was standing in the midst of the huge project, with the engineeer in charge next to him. All around them were "giant bulldozers, excavators, tractors and construction machinery of every shape and make." Gangs of native laborers under the direction of European supervisors were everywhere at work. It was in short one of those typical enormous construction projects with which most of us, at one time or another, have had some experience. But here in Ghana the work was almost at a standstill. The problem was one small, spindly tree, still growing right in the middle of the site; "that damn-silly tree," the chief engineer called it.

Pull it out, Neal said. They'd tried that already; they'd tried everything. What about all this heavy equipment? None of it did any good. Those who have seen trees yanked out summarily by the roots along our highways, may appreciate Neal's disbelief. But it was true. Nothing had been able to budge the little tree.

The foreman, a native of that part of the country, told them that the tree was the home of a powerful spirit who had taken a dislike to the project. He advised them to get a fetish priest to deal with the spirit. The engineer, a European, was "annoyed" at this explanation of his problem, but finally agreed that the priest should be sent for, much to Neal's surprise. Neal decided to stick around to see what happened.

The priest arrived and agreed to help. He stipulated that three sheep and three bottles of gin be brought forward as gifts for the spirit, and a £100 payment for himself, when the job should be completed. The engineer accepted these conditions, and the priest set to work. He sacrificed the sheep in such a manner that their blood drained into the ground at the foot of the tree. He also poured on some of the gin, and then went into his trance, during which he conversed with the spirit. Neal, standing by in amused incredulity, had an assistant translate for him. The priest was explaining the worthiness of the port project to the spirit, he learned.

After his explanations, the priest poured out the rest of the gin, made some further ceremony, and turned to the chief engineer. The spirit, he said, had agreed to leave and make his house in another and even better tree.

"Thank you very much," Simmons replied. "We'll put steel cables round it again and try to hoist it up with tractors and bulldozers."

"There is no need for that now, O Master," the Fetish Priest replied. "Let your foreman put a rope round the tree, O Master, and let a few men help him to pull it. It will come out without trouble."

Neal was by this time, he tells us, "very close to amusement." He thought the African a "con-man" and the engineer a "gullible idiot"—or at least, that they would soon prove to be so. He was dumfounded when, after "a preliminary tug" on the rope, "the tree came away, leaned over, and lay on the ground, its tangle of roots pointing grotesquely in all directions."[1]

There are, of course, a number of ways to interpret this story. The man who reports it, James Neal, may be, or may have been, himself a gullible idiot, or a con-man. He may be the familiar occultist quack, steeped in esoteric lore, ripe to believe anything; or on the other hand, a rogue, a crook who knows how to dress up a story for a publisher. In fact he seems to be neither. As to his credentials as occultist, he looks and acts far more like the typical civil servant. He was graduated from the School of Accountancy, the Polytechnic College in London. He has been in Her Majesty's government as a Chief Accountant and Financial Advisor, and has served abroad in the same capacity, in Palestine and Mauritius. The face which looks at us from the book-jacket photograph is one which would not be out of place at the head table of a Rotary or Kiwanis Club luncheon.

As to roguery, we have good reason not to suspect him of that either, since, as his book tells us, he was eventually seriously injured as a consequence of his broils with the West-African witch doctors, so seriously that he had to leave his job and go into retirement in England. While superintending an arrest from the top of a grandstand with no one near him, he was suddenly pushed over the edge. Witnesses bore out his impression that there was nobody within sixty feet of him but for all that he sustained multiple fractures of the left arm, left leg, and side.

A better avenue of inquiry into the case might concern itself with Neal's unconscious acceptance of African ways of thought, his unwitting participation in the dominant psychic life of Ghana. He had lived there ten years. Because he knew that powerful opponents wished him ill, and had resorted to black magic against him, did he accept, as Africans do, the inevitability of mischance? Did he throw himself over the top of the grandstand? Was his system infiltrated by drugs, so that he became unusually susceptible to suggestion? Or have African magicians, as many believe, actually mastered a technique of telekinesis?

These questions and others, applied to similar cases ranging over hundreds of years, will be the chief work of this book. Witchcraft is a complex subject, and has evoked complex responses from many disciplines. There are theological, historical, philosophical, anthropological, legal, literary, pharmacological, and psychological theories of witchcraft, to name some of the major ones. That is the reason why few people today can agree on what witchcraft really is, or was, or what witches really did, or what they do.

To return to Neal's case, which is one of thousands available to us: what does *he* think happened to him? It is clear that he has accepted, after initial resistance, the idea that he was the victim of a supernatural assault. And what was the agency of this assault? The subtitle of his book is "my life among the witch doctors of West Africa." But the Africans in question do not call themselves witches. Their word for the system of illicit supernatural or "paranormal" activity which first astounded and later harassed Neal, is "ju-ju."

The principle is an important one. "Witchcraft" would seem to be a European term of opprobrium which has been used in scatter-gun fashion for all sorts of threatening manifestations, whether at home or abroad. The major question is, does it work for us or against us? "Voodoo," for example, is a religion which inspires horror in most Americans, but explained by one of its own priests it seems no more formidable than Presbyterianism. Some of our Christian sects might well inspire distaste and even fear in those not so well acquainted with them as we are. "Witchcraft" is a term which has over several centuries been flung at a large number of undesirables of widely varying credentials.

During the height of the witchcraft scare in Europe, the sixteenth and seventeenth centuries, almost anything strange and fearful was attributed to witchcraft. A good example is the phenomenon called the poltergeist, which will be considered in some detail in a later chapter. Briefly, the poltergeist, which typically manifests itself in crude, uproarious disturbances of one kind or another—rappings, bangings (the name means "rapping spirit"), overturned furniture and other hi-jinks, now appears to be approachable as a neurotic symptom. Psychoanalysts, the best known among them being Nandor Fodor, have had success in dealing with poltergeist "hauntings" by applying psychiatric techniques to the victims.[2] There is no particular reason to attribute these phenomena to baleful influences, much less to witches, but they were nonetheless usually so attributed in the seventeenth century, as in the case of the Drummer of Tedworth, recorded by Joseph Glanvil in 1700.[3] Less remarkable, and infinitely more common, than poltergeists, were the ordinary illnesses and aggravations of domestic life, any one of which might be conveniently explained by reference to witchcraft. "The atomic bomb" serves many a citizen in a similarly useful way in my section of the country at present, as do "flying saucers."[4]

On the other hand, it is worthwhile considering some of the conventionally inexplicable manifestations which have occurred *in support of* such favored bodies as the Christian church, Charlemagne's army, or the children of Israel. Joshua's capture of Jericho, for example, was effected by superhuman power—but that power was Divine, not demonic (Josh. 6). The opinion of the citizens of Jericho, however, is not upon record. An even better example from the Old Testament is the plagues of Egypt, which though effected by Jehovah on behalf of His people, bear a striking resemblance to crimes alleged against witches in countless trials. The plague of insect pests for example—a common charge against witches; even worse, visitations of frogs! If these had been toads, the parallel would have been perfect. And finally, the slaughter of the Egyptians' first-born by indirect agency: under different circumstances, pure *maleficia*, to use the terminology evolved by the witch-hunters (Exod. 7-12).

It is appropriate, and inevitable, that our inquiry should have brought us to the Bible. For while it is false to say, as some writers have, that the witch persecutions were carried on solely by the church, it is nevertheless undeniable that historical witchcraft received its definition from the church. In a sense it may be said that witchcraft as a system was created by the church. *Convenience* again may be cited: it was convenient for the church to lump its own heresies, rival systems of faith, inexplicable spiritual phenomena—in fact, almost all the threats to its own primacy—into a single opposition, which in the slow course of many centuries took on the shape of a hostile conspiracy and the name of witchcraft. The church had, after all, ready to hand the Supreme Enemy of Man, Satan, acknowledged as the father of all error, the prince of the world's vanities, and arch rebel against God. There was no fault of logic involved in placing him at the source of trouble. Thus both the Knights Templars and Mohammed were identified as his servants working under his orders to subvert the church. And on an everyday scale, his designs might be traced in all sorts of unhappy and mysterious occurrences—failure of a churn, illness in cattle or men, a spell of bad weather. It did not happen all at once, but over hundreds of years: eventually the church, with all its contending motives and internal conflicts, came to identify witchcraft as a heresy against God, a supreme crime. With this formulation, which began to take shape in the fourteenth century, the witch mania and its attendant persecutions were inevitable; it remained only for the laity, especially the lawyers, to work out the details.

This is the classical definition of witchcraft: a literally diabolic plot against mankind. For long ages it was almost universally accepted. Running concurrently with it was what we may identify as the skeptical position: that the whole thing was nonsense, and an outrageous calumny on the loving nature of the Deity. This is an honorable and attractive position, and one which is still dominant today. It can trace its origins to a tiny handful of brave men during the Renaissance, men like Reginald Scot and Johan Weyer, who were in considerable danger for their beliefs. These ideas however gradually won out, by the eighteenth century, and were elevated almost beyond argument by the busy and progressive nineteenth. Today they are coming under renewed question.

The principal contribution of the twentieth century to witchcraft studies thus far is the theory which has been advanced from what we may call the anthropological position.[5] It states that the orthodox definition was in essence correct, although not in its details: that there actually did exist, in competition with the church, a rival system of faith which the church pledged itself to destroy. This was the fertility religion identified in such detail by Sir James Frazer as occurring at a certain level of development in all cultures. In Europe this religion continued to exert a major influence over the masses, the theory holds, through the so-called Christian Middle Ages and right up into the fourteenth century when the church, feeling itself strong enough for the first time, began the head-on confrontation which eventually resulted in the extirpation of the Old Religion, as Margaret Murray calls it. It was Murray, working from positions supported by Frazer, who first advanced this theory, in *The Witch-Cult in Western Europe* (Oxford, 1921), and elaborated it in *The God of the Witches* (London, 1931). Her findings inspired a number of followers, who for a time seemed likely to become the dominant party in witchcraft studies. They have within the last several decades, however, been greatly reduced in importance, because of renewed attacks by skeptics such as H. C. Lea, whose studies were published posthumously in 1939 as *Materials Toward a History of Witchcraft;* George Lincoln Burr and C. L. Ewen; and latterly E. E. Rose, Rossell Hope Robbins, whose prestigious *Encyclopedia of Witchcraft and Demonology* appeared in 1959, and Norman Cohn, to name just a few.

In the meantime other schools were rising; nor can it be assumed that the orthodox party, if we can call it that, was silenced. On the contrary it lived on in the person of the redoubtable Montague Summers, sometime priest, disciple of the inquisitors and Cotton Mather, antiquarian, critic, poet, short story writer, and major witchcraft scholar. His bibliography lists over three hundred items, the majority perhaps on occult subjects. He was also an indefatiguable republisher of old texts, which he furnished with introductions carrying all the freight of his erudition.

A fourth major party in witchcraft studies also had its origins in the earliest days of the persecutions: this is the psychological school, which may be said to have come into being with the first priestly doubts as to the sanity of some of those under arraignment.[6] It was given tremendous impetus by the revelations of Freud, Jung, and Adler, and continues to break ground in many important areas. Thus, the early twentieth century advances in understanding the true nature of hysteria and dissociative states are now being carried to their natural limits: that the human brain itself and alone is capable of producing all the varied phenomena which we call "the supernatural." All occult phenomena are then in some sense the products of psychic dysfunction—haunting is another kind of paranoia. This is not the same thing as saying, as some of our ancestors did, that these phenomena are all illusion, that they do not occur. Rather, the new psychology approaches them as it would the psychosomatic disorders, like ulcers: they are certainly real, and painful, but they may be produced by the mind, even in such solid shape as to be perceived by disinterested spectators. I have already alluded to the work of Nandor Fodor. But his findings and those of his colleagues are as yet by no means beyond question; many are still in the experimental stage.

A predictable corollary would be the emergence of a pharmacological or chemical school, which would stress a physiological approach to the problem. If the mind influences the body, the body can influence the mind. In fact such a school has arisen and is becoming strong. The earliest records show a connection between witches and drugs; our society, drug conscious as never before, is the first in years to take these early records seriously. There was a scattering of interest in the subject in the first decades of the twentieth century: Dr. H. J. Norman contributed a learned but tentative essay called "Witch Ointments" as an appendix to Summers' *The Werewolf* (London, 1933); and Langdon-Brown dealt with the subject more fully in his unfortunately little-known book, *From Witchcraft to Chemotheropy* (Cambridge, 1941). This information, together with many new findings of the toxicologists, was being assembled by George N. Conklin, a brilliant scholar whose early death put an end to any prospect of the definitive book he might have written. He did however publish a short but vitally important article on the subject called "Alkaloids and the Witches' Sabbath," in the May 1958 issue of the *American Journal of Pharmacy* (130:171-74).

In recent years, with interest in drugs mounting enormously, and with the high popularity of such various investigators into their effects as Aldous Huxley, Robert Graves, Timothy Leary, and Allen Ginsberg, this aspect of witch studies has become important. Anthropologists such as Michael Harner became convinced from their work with South American cultures, that a whole new pharmacological approach to European witchcraft was needed. A fictionalized treatment of these and related matters, Peter Matthiessen's *At Play in the Fields of the Lord* (New York, 1965) was well received; the big book as the seventies opened was Carlos Castaneda's *The Teachings of Don Juan* (Los Angeles, 1968).

Related to this school and the main anthropological body is the group which I call the transcendentalists. They agree with the anthropologists that witches were adherants to a pre-Christian faith, but go further in claiming still to adhere to that faith. They could be dealt with as an offshoot of the anthropologists, but it seems to me that they have adopted a postion which must stand by itself. After all, one may easily enough believe in the survival of pagan religions without declaring one's self to be a member of such a religion. In fact, anthropologists might argue that the triumph of the church in the late seventeeth century meant the extirpation of the true cult. Nevertheless Margaret Murray provided an introduction to *Witchcraft Today* (London, 1954), the apologia of Gerald B. Gardner, recognized until his recent death (1964) as chief among the witches of Great Britain.

Needless to say, the claims of this group are open to serious question, particularly if the skeptics are right; it will be recalled that they deny any actual system of belief, any true religion held by a majority of witches. Moreover, as any mediaevalist will point out, our knowledge of the details of actual daily life during the Middle Ages is pitifully sparse; how is it then that present-day witches can claim unbroken lines of descent with such complacency? Nevertheless some of them do, and many more have signed up with them as converts. The transcendental school, led by such colorful personalities as Sybil Leek, and given good coverage on television and in glossy autobiographies, has created a great stir which shows no sign of abatement.

My final category is one which I call the Occultists. According to these people, all of our science and religion has gone astray, and has been so for years. The truth about the human condition is more complex, they report, than most of us can grasp; but basically they adhere to the pre-Copernican, pre-Newtonian universe. Theirs is a world peopled with elementals—huge entities brooding over our daily life, who may inadvertently or by design be brought to meddle in human affairs, usually with disastrous consequences. The spirits of the dead are everywhere about, and may indeed, as our ancestors thought, be summoned to parley, or made to reveal treasure. Actually, this group—a group only for my present convenience; in truth the loosest of confederacies—is closer to paganism than are most of the witchcraft cultists.

This school too is fertile in publication, although many of their productions are brushed aside by the scholarly world. This is the complaint of the last remaining followers of the once-famous Aleister Crowley, who hold him to be one of the greatest thinkers and artists of our time. Serious criticism remains on the whole deaf to these claims, but there are some signs of revival even here: a splendid new edition of Crowley's autobiography (New York, 1970), a reissued book of interpretation by Israel Regardie and P.

R. Stephensen, *The Legend of Aleister Crowley* (St. Paul, Minnesota, 1970) and a voluminous new study by Regardie, *The Eye In The Triangle* (St.Paul, 1970).

Others in this school who will repay study are Algernon Blackwood, whose fiction gives perhaps the best and surely the most entertaining picture of the beliefs of the group, particularly the stories about John Silence, "the psychic doctor"; and Elliott O'Donnell, a formidable writer who has published a whole series of investigations into England's ghosts. His *Werwolves (sic)* (New York, 1965) gives a thoroughly frightening if not entirely believable theory of the supernatural, supported by many eerie tales.

There are then at present at least seven major schools of witchcraft thought, some of them frankly hostile to the others: the orthodox, skeptical, anthropological, psychological, pharmacological, transcendental, and occultist. Small wonder that the beginner may puzzle over their conflicting claims. In this book I shall attempt to give each a fair hearing, although probably to the satisfaction of none of them; my consolation must be that I am writing not to change their opinions, which would probably be impossible, but to assist the student.

This brings us back to the gentleman with whom we began, that reluctant student J. H. Neal. When all is said and done, what *did* happen to him? Surveying our early findings, we shall have to summarize his own response as in the orthodox tradition, which might be somewhat surprising, considering the ground gained by the new schools. But his belief—that he was the victim of malicious magic directed against him by sorcerers in league with dark forces—is probably the first reaction of most people today who collide with these matters, and I mean most people in Europe and the United States. The anthropocentric universe dies hard; it has in fact never died, as we may determine by listening to the average person struck down by disease or traffic: "what did I do to deserve this?" Nevertheless the new schools press forward, eager to be of service, and we must attend to their claims. But our next chapter, if by seniority alone, belongs to the Devil.

2. Satan

There is no one, I suppose, who has inspired more great writing, and more poor writing, than the Devil. I do not mean that he is the proper muse to men of letters, although more than one writer has suggested as much, notably Blake, who made the famous remark that Milton, as a poet, was of the Devil's party without knowing it.[1] Whatever the truth of that assertion, Satan simply as subject matter has an impressive place in literature. Almost every great writer makes at least one bow to him: Chaucer, Dante, Shakespeare, Machiavelli, Marlowe (although calling him by various names), until with *Paradise Lost* he achieves the status of epic hero, certainly the great role of his early literary career. The eighteenth century paid markedly less attention to him, until at its close he made his appearance in the dubious company of the Gothic novelists. The Romantics in general treated him with a familiarity which sometimes descended to coarseness, as with Burns, who addressed him as "Nick", "Clootie" and "auld horney."[2] Blake upheld his majesty to a certain degree, although his intentions were clearly ironic (in the Blakean universe angels are devils and devils are angels); but the lesser writers tousled him about unmercifully. In the best that the *schauerromantik* school can provide, he is usually wooden and predictable, as in *The Monk;* wildly improbable, as in the juvenilia of Shelley *(Zastrozzi, St. Irvine);* or contemptuously dismissed, as in *Manfred.* The greatest English Romantic master of horror, Beddoes, has little to say about him, unfortunately. Even Goethe takes away most of his power. He does achieve billing over Southey in Byron's *Vision of Judgment,* however, and Scott glances at him here and there (most celebratedly in *Redgauntlet).*

Victorian small-fry such as Barry Cornwall, Hood, Jerrold and Barham *(The Ingoldsby Legends),* aided by the genius of

Cruikshank, Hablot Browne and other caricaturists, continued the downgrading trend, but a reversal was inevitable, and the giants of the later century reestablished Satan on his throne of fire: Stevenson, Poe, Dostoyevsky, Balzac, Maupassant, Gogol, Hawthorne. The *fin de siecle* did not diminish his glory—"Enoch Soames" alone is worth fifty of those Gothic effusions so well described by Wordsworth: "frantic novels, sickly and stupid German tragedies, and deluges of idle and extravagant stories in verse."[3]

As with most things, our time has perpetuated the best and worst of the past: we have given the world masterpieces like Mikhail Bulgakov's *The Master and Margarita* side by side with potboilers like *Rosemary's Baby*. One thing is sure: whether we believe in Satan or not, we have never forgotten him. He figures as prominently, I should guess, in our doings and sayings, as he has ever done. Like our ancestors, we are willing to put the responsibility for all of our misdeeds upon him, much to the disgust of the infernal regions, if we may believe Saki, who quotes this speech from the Hellish Parliament: "If one investigates such statements as 'inhuman treatment of pit ponies' or 'fiendish cruelties in the Congo'. . . .one finds accumulative and indisputable evidence that it is the human treatment of pit ponies and Congo natives that is really in question."[4]

Satan, who is now so much, started out as no one at all. Like "Minos," or "Pharaoh," the name signified a title, not a person. Any angel in God's court could fill the office of "Satan," which meant "adversary." A "Satan" functioned much like a prosecutor, as we learn from the Old Testament. The most famous appearance in this work of such a functionary occurs in the Book of Job. There Satan is identified as an adversary, but not an adversary of God. He is one of the "sons of God" (angels)—"Now there was a day when the sons of God came to present themselves before the Lord, and Satan came also among them" (1:6). The point is, that as God considers the case of Job, who appears to have no faults, Satan functions as his prosecuting attorney, an officer of the court, bound to its rules like everyone else; not hostile in the least to the judge, but rather hoping to convince him of the superiority of his own arguments. The celebrated theme of the book, the origin of suffering in the world, gains considerably in richness and subtlety from an appreciation of this detail: it is not a case of one God being duped by a rival God into injuring his own worshiper, but rather the Deity Himself pondering upon His creation in the full splendor and panoply of His own excellence.[5]

There are other instances, even more illuminating, in the Old Testament. In Num. 22:22, the story of Balaam's ass, God, angry at Balaam, sends an angel to oppose his flight. "And God's anger was kindled because he went; and the angel of the Lord stood in the way for an adversary against him." The word is *Satan;* God orders one of his angels to become a satan to Balaam. Likewise in 1 Chron. 21:1, God sends a satan to provoke David to number Israel (a sin in the eyes of the Lord): "And Satan stood up against Israel and provoked David to number Israel."[6]

By the time of the New Testament, however, this is changed. Whether the advent of the God of love meant a concomitant personification and intensification of evil or, more simply, whether the office rendered the officer odious, as in the case of the hangman, the position of Satan has hardened, focussed into a personality. This phenomenon is of crucial importance to any study of witchcraft, because witchcraft, in its orthodox and commonly understood definition, literally could not exist without a personalized principle of evil. The whole witchcraft belief is based upon this active principle of evil, which is abroad, and to which one may pledge one's services. The great and greatly appalling handbook of the inquisitors, the *Malleus Maleficarum* (1486), begins its thousand arguments with this statement: "Malleus Maleficarum / The first part treating of the three necessary concomitants of witchcraft, which are the devil, a witch, and the permission of Almighty God."[7]

Our Lord clearly thought of Satan as a personal opponent and his disciples invariably spoke of him in this way also. Luke, in his tenth chapter, tells how Jesus sent forth seventy of his disciples to heal the sick; they return jubilant, saying "even the devils are subject unto us through thy name." And Jesus says, "I beheld Satan as lightning fall from heaven." This remark was to be the foundation of much theorizing among the Fathers; at the least it seems to indicate Jesus', and man's, triumph over the Enemy;

Satan's chagrin at the disciples' success.

John (16:11) speaks of "the prince of this world," apparently meaning Satan, for we have been previously assured that the things of this world are in Satan's keeping, in texts which we shall consult shortly; Paul, to the Ephesians (2:2), links "this world" to "the prince of the power of the air, the spirit that now worketh in the children of disobedience." Satan is gathering attributes of mystery, power and majesty unto himself from the midst of the godly, a trend greatly accelerated among the Fathers and the mediaeval church. The great confrontation of Jesus and Satan of course, is that of the Wilderness, reported by both Matthew (4), and Luke (4). These accounts agree closely in their drama and brevity, varying only in the order of the three temptations. Both point out that "the devil" appeared to Jesus when he was hungry and tired, urging him to change stones to bread. Milton follows Luke in making the last temptation that of the pinnacle of the temple: "if thou be the Son of God, cast thyself down from hence." The episode becomes the climax of *Paradise Regained*, Milton investing it with a greatly enlarged significance: "So after many a foil the Tempter proud, / Renewing fresh assaults, amidst his pride / Fell when he stood to see his Victor fall" (4.569-71).

The other temptation, which Matthew makes the last, is that of all the kingdoms of the world. The devil offers to give them to Jesus in return for his fealty, but Jesus rebukes him, saying, "Get thee hence, Satan: for it is written, thou shalt worship the Lord thy God, and him only shalt thou serve" (Matt. 4:10). Here is a firm foundation for Satan's preeminence in our world, a preeminence granted to him for many centuries of Christian thought, and, if perhaps only metaphorically, still retained by him today.

Our last example of Satan's progress in the New Testament is taken from Revelation, the famous passage describing war in heaven:

> And there was war in heaven: Michael and his angels fought against the dragon; and the dragon fought and his angels,
>
> And prevailed not; neither was their place found any more in heaven.
>
> And the great dragon was cast out, that old serpent, called

the Devil, and Satan, which deceiveth the whole world: he
was cast out into the earth, and his angels were cast out
with him. (12.7-9)

The apocalypse is dangerous ground for the layman, and for
the clergy, too, if we may judge from the enormous structures
they have built on its uncertain surface. It seems safe to suppose
that most if not all of this material is metaphorical, and that it
has been handled as fact by commentators from the earliest
times. Much witchcraft lore depends upon literal readings of
figurative passages in the Bible and elsewhere, as we shall see.

The development of both Judaism and Christianity greatly
increased Satan's powers. The Apocrypha, particularly Tobit, and
other early texts, such as the Book of Enoch, the book of Jubilees,
and the Testaments of the Twelve Patriarchs, are storehouses of
demonic lore, wherein Satan and his followers are described
in enormous detail as to their appearances, histories, and
predilections. These too are dark regions and may not be safely
entered without a guide, like Lea (vol. 1) or Gustav Davidson,
author of the very helpful *Dictionary of Angels* (New York, 1967).
The student may also find Cecil Roth's *History of The Jews* useful
(New York, 1961, paperback). Among the important details first
proposed in early Christian and rabbinical writings, and later
developed and solidified by Christian theologians, are the
identification with Satan of the serpent in the garden of Eden (2
Esdras, ca. A.D. 80), and the Fall of the Angels (based on hints in
Scripture—Gen. 6:1-4; Isa. 24:21-22, and of course the Revelation
passage quoted above, and greatly developed in Enoch [ca. 125
B.C.] as well as the later Jubilees and the Twelve Patriarchs).

Most significant of all, the number of Satan's legions was greatly
increased, even as he himself was magnified. As he gained
followers, he also took on new *personae*, new incarnations by the
score. One of the earliest and most important of these was his
identification with Lucifer. This would seem to have come about
through a misreading of Isaiah by Origen (ca.A.D. 185-254), but
whatever the truth of the matter, the idea was congenial to the early
church. In his fourteenth chapter, Isaiah prophesies with
considerable satisfaction the downfall of a powerful prince whom,

following a practice still current, he identifies as a great luminary:

> How art thou fallen from heaven, O Lucifer, son of the
> morning! how art thou cast down to the ground, which
> didst weaken the nations!

> For thou hast said in thine heart, I will ascend into heaven,
> I will exalt my throne above the stars of God: I will sit also
> upon the mount of the congregation, in the sides of the
> north:

> I will ascend above the heights of the clouds; I will be like
> the most High.

> Yet thou shalt be brought down to hell, to the sides of the
> pit. (12-15)

It seems evident to us that Isaiah is referring to the king of
Babylon, whom he mentions at the outset of his chapter (verse 4);
but given the temper of the early church, or perhaps we ought to
say, the human temperament, the more sensational reading was
inevitable. It fits so perfectly with the text in Revelation, for one
thing.

The word *devil* enters the picture in the third century, with the
Septuagint translation of the Old Testament into Greek (so-called
because of the tradition that it was written in 70 or 72 days by 70
or 72 men), for Ptolemy of Egypt. The Greek word *diabolos—
accuser*—was at that time chosen as a fitting translation for the Hebrew *Satan*. Thus in the Greek Old Testament *Satan* became *diabolos;* and when the translation was made to Latin, the word took on
its Latin form, *diabolus*, which is the origin of *devil, teufel, deil, dia-
ble*, and all the other well-known variations. Jerome restored the
word *Satan* to the Vulgate, except for psalm 109.

This was well enough for the Old Testament, but in the New, as
we have seen, Satan had become a different sort of figure, an
opponent of God rather than a God-appointed opponent of man.
The two different entities might almost have been translated into
two different words, but of course they were not, and so the idea
became firmly implanted that Satan—the devil—had always been
an enemy of God from the earliest times.

But besides the Devil, Satan, there were also "devils—"unclean spirits," hostile influences which were everywhere and might take possession of man, woman or child. Jesus had many confrontations with these. Furthermore, to the embarrassment of some modern commentators, He distinguished carefully between ordinary sickness and demonic possession. As Monsignor Catharinet puts it, writing in the anthology *Satan*, which is the best and most comprehensive study available in our time, "The attitude of Jesus in the presence of the possessed does not allow a Catholic, nor even any attentive historian, to think that in acting and speaking as He did He was merely accommodating Himself to the ignorances *[sic]* and prejudices of His contemporaries."9 Of course, all these "unclean spirits" were lumped together as "devils," members of Satan's host, sent on his orders to torment his enemy, man. The elements of the demonic conspiracy were at hand.

The word *demon* itself, just used, provides yet another example of the acquisitive nature of the Adversary. Originally this word, *daemon* in Greek, while properly applied to a spiritual being, had nothing to do with Satan and his hosts, nor indeed any evil principle. It signified a guardian spirit, or spirit of inspiration; a spiritual manifestation or intensification, that is to say, of one's own individuality. Shakespeare uses the word this way in *Antony and Cleopatra* (2.3.19), as does Shelley in *Alastor* and Keats in his "Ode on Indolence"—"my demon poesy" (1.40). But the Septuagint Bible used this word for the Hebrew "Schedim"—"vengeful idols"; and "seirim"—"hairy satyrs," which are mentioned in 2 Chron. as the abominations brought upon the people of Israel by Rheoboam (supposedly a reference to Pan-worship introduced from Egypt), 11:15. "Satyrs" are mentioned by Isaiah (13:21) also, but the creatures in Chronicles are simply called "devils" in the King James version. So *demon* and *devil* became interchangeable. Furthermore, the word demon was used in the Septaugint for the *destroyer* mentioned in the book of Tobit in the Apocrypha (6:14; 8:3).

Then John Wycliffe, who translated the Bible into English in the fourteenth century, had, in casting round for a suitable translation for *Satan*, hit upon the apt expression *fiend*, an old word simply meaning *enemy*. This word too was quickly caught up in the muddle: today, having totally lost its original meaning, it is synonymous with *demon* and *devil*—with perhaps a slight advantage in terror because of its archaic savor.

"All these terms," as Robbins puts it, "devolved upon Satan, who absorbed into himself all biblical references to any enemy of God."[10] These and many others; and many other personalities, other gods, warriors, even animals, became associated with the Devil. It has long been remarked that the gods of a conquered people become the devils of their conquerors. Sometimes this problem is solved by having one of the conquered gods born again, into the new order, as in the celebrated case of Athena, born parthenogenetically into the Olympian pantheon as favorite daughter of Zeus. More often, however, as in the case of Baal, a great rival of Jehovah, the deposed god becomes a devil, a subversive, a guerrilla fighter; his worship is hostile to church and state and must be rooted out. Thomas Lovell Beddoes puts it memorably: "ruined angels straight become fiends."[11] To get rid of them is not easy. According to one school, this difficult process is the story of the witchcraft persecutions.

We have already noted the confusion of Satan with Lucifer. Also very early was Satan's identification with Beelzebub, or Baalsebub, "the Lord of the flies"—his name has many variations. He is clearly one of the manifestations of Baal, "God" or "Lord" in Syrian. In the Old Testament he is a rival deity (2 Kings 1): "Baalzebub the god of Ekron." But in the New, he is "the prince of the devils" (Mark 3:22). In that same passage, however, he is identified with Satan, by Jesus himself; Jesus has been accused of casting out devils by the aid of Beelzebub, but He says, "How can Satan cast out Satan?" (3:23). Of course the confusion was inevitable; there cannot be two supreme princes of evil. Dante follows this tradition and identifies Beelzebub with Satan. Yet Beelzebub's individuality reasserts itself: Milton solves the problem by placing him second in command. Today he is generally considered a separate personality, one of considerable majesty and force.

Another great lord in the hellish hierarchy is Mephistopheles, to use the common spelling (as usual there are many others). His name derives from the Hebrew: "mephiz" = "destroyer," and "tophel" = "liar," according to Gustav Davidson.[12] He would seem to have been a god of Akkad, although he plays no part in Scripture. His role in secular literature is a major one, however; he will be remembered as one of the principals in the Faust legend. In Goethe, he is second in command to Satan; in Marlowe, to Lucifer, "arch-regent and commander of all spirits" (1.3).

Asmodeus is another devil of rank so exalted that he is frequently confused with Satan. Davidson derives his name from the Persian "ashma daeva" = "creature of judgment,"[13] but Ludwig Couard (cited by Lea) argues for a Hebrew origin: "asmod" = "destroyer."[14] Whatever his origins, Asmodeus has had a distinguished career in evil; it was he who slew the seven bridegrooms in the book of Tobit, and he who got Noah drunk, according to demonologists quoted by Davidson[15] (there is, however, no scriptural authority for this accomplishment: see Gen. 9:20-29). He is the hero of Le Sage's *The Devil On Two Sticks*, first published in 1707, and continued by several hands; he is cited by Byron as lieutenant and favorite of Satan in *The Vision of Judgment;* and he figures prominently in a book by James Branch Cabell, *The Devil's Own Dear Son* (1949).

There are thousands of other devils; two or three more are worthy of notice here. One is certainly Apollyon, who is well known to scripture. His name is the Greek form of the Hebrew "Abaddon" = "destroyer." Both his names are mentioned in Rev. 9:11, where he is identified as "the angel of the bottomless pit." In the twentieth chapter of this book, second verse, he is said to have "laid hold on the dragon, that old serpent, which is the Devil, and Satan, and bound him a thousand years." So that here, like Satan himself in better days, he is conceived of as an officer of the Lord. Yet, like Satan, he was corrupted by his office; perhaps the reasoning ran that, as he was in the bottomless pit, he must have deserved to be there. At any rate, we find him degenerating rapidly in early noncanonical writings until, in his most famous appearance in literature, Bunyan's *Pilgrim's Progress*, he is identified as the Devil himself. The final indignity came to him in the nineteenth century when the eccentric demonologist Francis Barrett (*The Magus*, London, 1801) separated his Hebrew and Greek identities;

Abaddon and Apollyon are usually considered two different devils today.

Another case of mistaken identity exists between Belial and Beliar, who have down through the centuries become hopelessly confused. Belial is perhaps better known at present, because of Paul's question, "what concord hath Christ with Belial?" (2 Cor. 6:15). Apparently Paul wishes to signify a polar opposition in this remark, and therefore we may assume Belial and Satan to have been interchangeable, at this particular time at least. Beliar, however, has the better canonical stance: he appears in Deuteronomy, Judges, and 1 Samuel as a symbol of evil. His name signifies "worthless."

The Devil, then, has many attributes, many names, many faces, many followers. Nevertheless a certain consistent image of him established itself with our ancestors: a black man; or a red man; talons, cloven hooves, horns, and tail. This is not the Scriptural version. "The concept of the Christian Devil," according to Robbins, "was largely fixed by the so-called desert fathers, the hermits of the Egyptian deserts, in the third and fourth centuries, who pieced together from their hallucinations and recollections of replaced gods (such as the cloven-footed Pan) the visualization of the Devil as the grotesque man illustrated in the plates in this *Encyclopedia*."[16]

That is undoubtedly true; there is however much more to the matter than that. The anthropological writers will have their own chapter in this book, but it should be noted here that Satan's animal attributes are easily explained in light of their findings. However little faith one puts in Margaret Murray, one recognizes that many of the cults and religious remnants that Christianity was most opposed to bore the signs of animal-identification, animal-worship, and animal-sacrifice. The frank sexuality of these cults, most of them dedicated to promote fertility (or, as some say of the witches, to repress it), was repugnant to the church, with its strong emphasis on chastity and denial. Without doubt it came to look upon evil, to a certain extent, in the image of its predecessors.

All the evidence points to a strong theological need—and thus, a strong psychological need—for an active, formidable power of evil. Certainty of evil is apparently preferable to metaphysical indecision. But the dangers are many; God may not be involved in evil. The Devil may work with His permission, to bring about good beyond mankind's comprehension. This idea itself has often proved too subtle for men, as witness the strength of Manicheeism. This once-powerful faith, called a Christian heresy by the Church, had a basis in common sense that was, to many, unshakeable. The world is the battleground of contending powers; one bad, one good. They are of equal strength, so the issue is in doubt. The just man, who will wish to adhere to the good, has many ways of doing so; but he knows that he brings upon himself, by his virtuous behavior, the enmity of the evil powers. It must have been a satisfying religion; there is some doubt whether Christianity is free of it yet.

But this is to treat too casually a faith which, according to one of its students, "exercised an influence for more than a thousand years, upon the lives of countless numbers of devoted followers, inspired by the ideals and high principles of its founder, whom they accounted as divine."[17] Mani, the founder, was an enlightened and humane man. He despised war and categorically opposed it in his doctrine; rather, drawing upon the teachings of Zoroaster, Jesus, and Buddha, his avowed models, he propounded a religion given over to love for God and man. In a universe convulsed with the struggle between darkness and light, there is a special role for men, every one of whom is endowed with a spark of light, which is his hope of salvation. He can assure it for himself, and contribute to the downfall of evil, by purity of thought, word, and deed. Moreover Mani was a meliorist: he taught that it was possible and even inevitable, if men showed good faith, for the light to be liberated finally from encircling darkness.

What this represents is an early and inspired attempt to found a new religion upon the best of Eastern and Western philosophies. For his efforts Mani received the usual reward of the religious innovator: he was shunned, despised, abused, and finally butchered. But his religion made sense to the ordinary people, who clung to it stubbornly for centuries. The official attempts to induce them to relinquish it, with all the accompaniment of fire and sword, play a part in the story of witchcraft: as Professor Taraporewala says, "The last record of this religion is found among the Albigenses in Southern France, who were ruthlessly massacred by the orthodox

Catholics there."[18] And, I may add, accused of sorcery and demon-olatry. The slaughter of the Albigensians was the prelude to the persecutions of the witches, and both massacres were excused by the Church on the same grounds.

A religion which granted even more than parity to Satan—which, in fact, avowedly worshiped, and still does worship him as the god of this world—is that of the Yezidees. I was amused recently to find this comment upon the Yezidees in a book I was reviewing:

> Yes, there are actual black magic cults of men and women devoted to the worship of the devil. They are called Satanists. I have been told that the largest existing body of true devil-worshippers is the Yezidees of the Near East, but I presume it would be next to impossible to learn anything factual about them.[19]

That is a convenient presumption for the researcher. Actually, aside from the ordinary religious encyclopedias, there is a short but excellent article on the Yezidees in the anthology *Satan*, mentioned above, written by Louis Massignon. But by far the most interesting account of them I know is given by William Seabrook, who actually lived among them for a time, and probably came as close to their mysteries as any westerner has.[20]

This religion, according to Massignon, was also inspired by one who brought upon himself the hatred of orthodoxy "for his doctrine of deification by divine love." The position of Satan in Islam is a complex one; it is the orthodox view, as I understand it, that he "incurred damnation by his jealous and exclusive love of the pure idea of the deity." Orthodox Moslem thought therefore identified the holy man, Hallaj, referred to above, as an associate or instrument of Satan. Other Moslem theologians, however, upon the grounds that love sanctifies, canonized both Satan and Hallaj. A religious order which venerates them, the 'Adawiya, was founded by Sheik 'Adi, who died in 1162. This is the religion of the Yezidees.[21]

Needless to say, this point of view was odious to the main body of Islam, which persecuted it with vigor. But it had taken hold of a body of the people, who, following the tradition which we have noticed, that this world was given over to Satan at an early period, thought it only prudent to pay its devotions to him. Seabrook found that they welcomed him, as a consequence of the fact that he spoke English, because the English had recently put a stop to the persecutions of their faith by their orthodox neighbors.

As he was making his way into their dominions, his guide, a professor named Mechmed Hamdi, coached him in proper Yezidee etiquette.

I would find the Yezidees trustworthy, he said, and hospitable, but there were certain things always to be remembered when among them which, if forgotten, could lead to serious trouble.

One must take care never to pronounce the name Shaitan (Satan) and must avoid the use of any words or syllables, whether in English, French, or Arabic, which could, by any chance, be mistaken for that word—such Arabic words, for instance, as *khaitan* (thread) and *shait* (arrow).[22]

A blunder here would mean more than mere embarrassment, as Seabrook learned; a Yezidee who hears the proper name of his god pronounced is bound by his faith to kill the offender, or if that should not be possible, himself. Like other ancient religions, Satan-worship considers the very name of the deity sacred, and guards it from profanation. Jehovah had such a sacred name, the "unpronounceable name of God." The Yezidees call their god "Melek Taos"—"angel peacock"—and may converse about him, using his name, as freely as Christians may about Jesus.

Another important taboo involves the color blue, which cannot be worn among the Yezidees without giving great offense—it is supposed to contain properties inimical to Satan. "Blue amulets and charms," Seabrook notes, "particularly blue beads, are worn universally among Moslems as a protection against devils and to ward off the evil eye."[23] Moreover one must never spit in a fire, or put out a match with one's foot, as fire is a sacred element to the Yezidees.

Seabrook's adventures among this fascinating people are well worth reading in their entirety; they form the last section of his book on Arabia. It may be worthwhile to quote one more passage here, relating to certain practical aspects of the faith, reported to Seabrook by an old priest with whom he had become friendly.

"Well, we, of course, also believe in God," he told me; "but our difference from all other religions is this—that we know God is so far away that we can have no contact with Him—and He, on his part, has no knowledge or interest of any sort concerning human affairs. It is useless to pray to Him or worship Him. He cares nothing about us.

"He has given the entire control of this world for ten thousand years to the bright spirit, Melek Taos, and Him, therefore, we worship. Moslems and Christians are wrongly taught that he whom we call Melek Taos is the spirit of evil. We know that this is not true. He is the spirit of power and the ruler of this world. At the end of the ten thousand years of his reign—of which we are now in the third thousand—He will reenter paradise as the chief of the Seven Bright Spirits, and all His true worshippers will enter paradise with him."[24]

In essence, this somewhat resembles the statements of some of the witches under examination; those questioned by de Lancre, for example: "Jeanne Dibasson, aged twenty-nine, told us that the sabbat was the true paradise, where there was more pleasure than she was able to express."[25]

Was the god of the Yezidees the same that the witches adored? Some scholars would have us think so. The best recent research, however, like that of Norman Cohn, which will be considered in a later chapter, makes it seem more doubtful than ever that there was a unified body of witches operating in mediaeval and Renaissance Europe. But in the minds of the persecutors at least, Satan's preeminence was assured.

Some of the deepest human impulses—to assign responsibility for mischance, to provide a rational framework for xenophobia and paranoia—are involved in the rise of Satan. The very process of rebellion against authority by which the typical adolescent carves out for himself a place in the world, certainly has contributed to the cult of the Arch-Rebel, whether he be called Satan, Set, Prometheus, or Faustus. Thus Satan is indeed always to hand, as the demonologists warned, less as a real presence than as an excuse, a rationalization, for mankind's nastiest tendencies. As the people of Salem said, in their recantation, Satan had deluded them indeed.

And, of course, for those who dislike and fear our sensual life, Satan remains convenient, because as ancient traditions attest, he is the prince of this world, and all things in it, good and bad. Between him and those who hate the kingdom of flesh there can never be peace.

3. Origins: Biblical, Classical, Patristic

So man created the Devil, out of a fear of his own happiness. But the Devil was no more capable of ruling this earth unassisted than God the Father of reigning alone in Heaven. It was the work of thousands of men, over hundreds of years, to define the kingdom of the Christian God, which eventually took the shape of something very much like the Roman Empire. These same men—the best thinkers and scholars of their times—also produced, partly as a by-product of their theology, but also partly out of a love for the subject in its own right, a definition of the kingdom of Hell, which quite logically emerged from their researches as a gigantic though vain imitation of God's kingdom, an ugly and contemptible parody of everything good. God had Heaven; Satan had Hell, and this earth. God had His angels; Satan had his. And God has His Church, with its priestly hierarchy; so the Devil must needs have his. The Devil's church was witchcraft, and its priests were witches.

"Thou shalt not suffer a witch to live." This line, which has cost the lives of hundreds of thousands of people, is probably the key biblical reference to witchcraft. It afforded the Fathers, and the lawyers, and the ordinary citizens of many centuries, a perfect proof that the Devil's establishment was not a figment of their imaginations, but a real conspiracy known to their ancestors from the remotest ages, and moreover, warned against by God himself, in Holy Writ. The injunction appears in Exodus, the eighteenth verse of the twenty-second chapter, along with many other commandments specifically and personally delivered by God to Moses. The first ten of these, which are written in chapter twenty, are the most famous, but those that follow, like this one, and that which commands "eye for eye, tooth for tooth, hand for hand, foot for foot" (21:24), were intended to be no less binding, nor were they considered so by our ancestors, at many different periods.

As usual the problem is in the translation: what did the author of Exodus mean, that our ancestors rendered as "witch"? The word is "Kashaph," which occurs at numerous places in the Old Testament, and is now understood to mean "poisoner," at least in this connection, as Reginald Scot pointed out in 1584 (*The Discovery of Witchcraft*, 6.1). It is in fact hard to improve on Scot's explication of this matter; he does not deny that witches may use, or indeed have used, poisons to harm people, but he points out that it is specifically poisoners against whom the children of Israel are enjoined in this passage. And he continues to prove that many authorities, including Paul, used the words "to bewitch" metaphorically, to signify what the Elizabethans called "to cosen," and what we might call to cheat, to fool, to take advantage of. Witchcraft, Scot says, is cosenage—a racket, a confidence game—and should indeed be punished, but only for what it is.[1] This opinion and others like it caused Scot's book to be burned publicly at James I's accession, but Scot himself was beyond the reach of James's indignation, having died several years before. The all-superceding King James Bible translated "Kashaph" as "witch."

There are many other references in the Old Testament to activities which were easy to combine under the heading of "witchcraft." Considered in this light, they make up a formidable list of precedents for the witchfinder. Some of the best known of these occur in Leviticus (19:26, "enchantment"; 19:31, "familiar spirits," "wizards"; 20:6, "familiar spirits," "wizards"; 27, "wizards"), and Deuteronomy, in which Moses warns Israel against "divination," "an enchanter, or a witch" (18:10), "or a charmer, or a consulter with familiar spirits, or a wizard, or a necromancer" (18:11) as well as "a prophet . . . that shall speak in the name of other gods" (18:20). Here the intention seems clearly to be against rival religions and their practitioners, as in the famous case in 1 Samuel, that of "the witch of Endor" (28).

Even in the King James version, which does not spare the use of the word, this woman is not called a witch, but rather "a woman that hath a familiar spirit." Such people had been rigidly put down by Saul, but in his need he consults one, in order to ask advice of Samuel, who actually appears: "I saw gods ascending out of the earth" (28:12).[2] Once again, the issue is between Jehovah and rival deities, or, more strictly, Jehovah and his servant Saul, who has been slack in executing His "fierce wrath upon Amalek" (18). Nor should we forget the struggle between the orthodox, priestly interpreters of God's will and their rivals, who operated outside the established religion and were therefore enchanters, wizards, abominations. These distinctions however were lost upon the popular mind, as indeed upon standard clerical opinion, both of which inevitably identified the woman of Endor as a witch.

Jezebel, too, that great biblical examplar of female perifidy, is called a witch: "the whoredoms of thy mother Jezebel and her witchcrafts" (2 Kings, 9:22). Her story is that of an attempt to supercede Jehovah with Baal, who, as we have noted, was translated at an early date into the Christian pandemonium as Beelzebub, and Belphagor, and others. It was an inescapable conclusion that his followers would be witches.

In the New Testament, the word *witchcraft* occurs just once, in Gal. 5:20, where it is condemned along with wrath, strife, murder, and other evils as "a work of the flesh." The Greek word is *pharmakeia—charm*, or *remedy*. Obviously the reference has nothing to do with witchcraft as a heresy against God, and yet of course it was so understood. Furthermore we shall do well to remember the New Testament emphasis on "unclean spirits," often translated or paraphrased as "devils." The witchfinders felt themselves as well supported by the New Testament as by the Old.

The Fathers and their successors, the men who explored Satan's kingdom with such thoroughness, did not spare to identify his followers in detail. Many shared in this work, but two are of crucial importance, in this as in so many aspects of the development of Christianity: Augustine and Aquinas.

It would have been more than surprising if these two had not incorporated into their systems the extravagant belief in the invisible world of evil which was the universal heritage of their times. Even so, we may say of Augustine that his credulity was extreme. Along with the attractive and persuasive warmth of his Christian conviction, and no doubt partly as a consequence of it, he shows an unusual consciousness of the depth of man's psychological and spiritual mysteries. Unfortunately he tends to ascribe much of the mysterious in the world to the agency of demons. Thus the chapter headings of the tenth book of *The City of God:* "9, of unlawful arts concerning the devil's worship, whereof Porphyry approves some, and disallows others"; "10, of theurgy that falsely promises to cleanse the mind by the invocation of devils"; "21, of the power given to the devils to the greater glorifying of the saints." His eighth book treats of such matters as "the qualities of airy spirits"; the ninth, in even greater detail, the nature of demons. The twelfth, among other things, explains certain scriptural references to the Devil, who does not lose anything in the process. And these are but a minute sampling of Augustine's discussions of the business. As Lea says, "His influence thus was in the last degree unfortunate, for he fully accepted all the superstitions of his age, both as to theurgic and goetic magic, and explained everything by the power of demons."[3]

Augustine and the much later Aquinas may well be called the Plato and Aristotle of Christian thought; as to the relation between them, Lea remarks, "Aquinas' perpetual references to St. Augustin show how powerful was Augustin's influence on medieval thought. When his utterance could be quoted, nothing more was required."[4] And Aquinas was, of course, far more the systematizer. What had been thrown off in the random compilation of *The City of God*, over some thirteen years, was gathered in, pruned, ordered, and fitted with a vast amount of other material into the great Synthesis.

And Aquinas too fully acquiesced in the earthly primacy of the powers of darkness. According to Robbins, he "notably influenced thinking in the five core areas of practical witchcraft."[5] These Robbins lists as "Sexual Relations with Devils," "transvection" (flight through the air by a demonic aid, as to the sabbat), "metamorphosis," "storm-raising," and "ligature" (rendering men and beasts incapable of carnal union). One may question whether the "core areas of practical witchcraft" should be restricted to five—does not "possession" have a place among them?—but Aquinas's part in defining and solidifying these concepts seems beyond argument. When, in the course of editing Lea's enormous compilations, Professor Howland has considered Aquinas, he leaves him with these words: "Later theologians and demonologists are content, for the most part, to quote Aquinas or to echo his views, and there is no need to repeat the unsavory details."[6]

The *Summa* itself deals exhaustively with demonology, as in part 1, chapter 4, which poses two major questions on the subject: question 63, "The malice of the angels with regard to sin," and 64, "The punishment of the Demons." The numerous articles into which these headings are divided explore the subject in detail, although without the spicy particulars so beloved of later demonologists. The closest Aquinas comes to these is in his academic disputations, particularly the "quaestiones de quolibet," the solemn disputations open to the public twice a year, at advent and lent. "These writings are not recordings of the actual disputations," *The New Catholic Encyclopedia* says, "but rather stylized compositions written by the master, in this case Aquinas, on the basis of scholastic performance."[7] There are twelve of these, as the *Encyclopedia* cautiously puts it, "traditionally ascribed to Aquinas"; and it is among this material that Robbins finds many of his examples of Aquinas's influence in the five core areas. Here Aquinas discusses the incubus demon, devils' power to carry men and women off through the air, witches' ability to change people into animals (by means, however, of illusion), ligature, and the evil eye. Since there is apparently some doubt as to Aquinas's authorship of these discourses, however, the student may as well stay with the *Summa*, which gives the witch-hunters all the authority that they could wish, as in 1.8. 109, "The Ordering of the Bad Angels," or 1.8. 114, "The assaults of the Demons." And we should remember Aquinas's command in part 2 of the *Summa*, that heretics should not only be excommunicated, but "slain justly out of hand" (2.11).[8]

If Augustine and Aquinas were, as many believe, the great architects of the infernal realm as defined by the Church, there were still many hundreds of lesser builders, electricians, carpenters, and plumbers who filled in the structure and made it livable. Some of these we shall need to mention in later chapters. For the moment however, we need go no further into theology to understand the perverse importance of the black arts of sorcery, demonolatry, and divination to Christianity. Early Jewish sacred writings tell of the gradual triumph of the God Jehovah over his rivals, who then lapse to the status of demons. Those people who for one reason or another continue to treat with these fallen divinities are declared anathema. Their efforts, however pious, are looked upon with indignation and horror. Their prayers become evil incantations, their ritual, sorcery, and all their service, blasphemy and filth. Christianity building upon these attitudes and this material eventually combines these devils and their followers into a great conspiracy called "witchcraft." That is part of the story.

But all religions seem to develop in much the same way. As well as a Jewish heritage, Western Europe and the Christian church have a classical heritage. Much of what we call "witchcraft" comes down from the other source; and because the Greeks and Romans created their demons and their sorcerers in much the same way that the children of Israel did, the two systems may be seen to reinforce each other. Thus the witchfinders could present an almost airtight case.

The principal source of what we call witchcraft among the Greeks may be found, in my opinion, in the fragments of the matriarchal religion of the Mediterranean which was largely subdued by "the patriarchal Hellenes who invaded Greece and Asia Minor early in the second millennium B.C., and challenged the power of the triple-goddess," to quote Robert Graves. [9] Here again we are in some difficulty; the exact nature of the matriarchal religion, or its extent, or even in some cases its very existence, are questions still in dispute among scholars. But there is good reason to think that mankind, in an early period of its self-consciousness, organizes its impulses of veneration around women, who are seen as the creators of human life, the male role in sexual reproduction not having been ascertained. Such a system of worship is widely thought to have existed in Southern Europe up until comparatively recent times—four or five thousand years—when it was gradually superceded by patriarchal invaders from the north and east. The various stages of its modification into the solidly patriarchal system observable among the classical Greeks are identified by Frazer and others as matrilineal sacred monarchy, patrilineal sacred monarchy, and finally the fully patriarchal system, in which religion and politics merge to form the State, somewhat as we comprehend it.

Presumably this system ripened especially in the so-called "cradle areas" of civilization, where economic factors were favorable. How were women able to maintain their ascendancy over men in this religious system, which carries as a central detail of its rites, male sacrifice at regular intervals? One answer is that the terms of the system were enforced by religious awe; and that men were not, presumably, subjected in all their activities to female supervision. On the contrary there is reason to suppose that hunting, warfare, and many of the arts—the dance, for example—were largely or exclusively male prerogatives. The women, however, retained command of the divine mysteries of generation, including agriculture. All this sheds a particular significance on the study of witchcraft. One can scarcely think of a trial which is not based upon some abuse of fertility, some attempt to thwart the generative process in men, animals, or plants. And the unusual antifeminine bias of the persecutions gains some explanation from these theories too; theoretically anyone could be a witch.[10]

It is necessary to go back to another point: who was the triple goddess of whom Graves speaks? With her, we enter the edifice of witchcraft by the front door. She was Hecate, known for centuries to all men as the very queen of the witches. So she is identified in *Macbeth*, for example (although almost certainly placed there by someone other than Shakespeare; most likely Middleton). The Romans knew her and feared her. In Lucian's *Philopseudes* she is described as "terrible to see, in the form of a woman, half a furlong high, snake-footed, snakes in her hair, a torch in her left hand, a mighty sword in her right."[11] Montague Summers, from whom I draw the preceding quotation, is a trustworthy exponent of the orthodox view of her. "Horror, fear, and darkness rapidly accumulated about her," he tells us:

> her statue of triple form, the queen of three worlds, Selene in heaven, Artemis on earth, Persephone in hell, stood at the crossroads, a haunted spot, where, according to Plato

(*Laws* 873b), might be thrown the corpse of the murderer after execution, unwept, unburied, the prey of daws and crows. Her rites were monstrous, but to be respected and revered; her worshippers were accursed, but to be dreaded and placated; her prayers blasphemy; her sacrifices impious and terrible. It was in truth the very cult of hell.[12]

Hecate has sunk very low, like Baal. Like him too she was formerly invested with divine honors, the difference being that some of her glory still clings to her in early texts. In Hesiod's *Theogony* she is identified as "The good mediator between mankind and The Gods" according to N. O. Brown.[13] Here is Hesiod's actual description of the goddess in the days of her greatness, as translated by Brown.

Asteria conceived and gave birth to Hecate, whom Zeus the son of Cronus exalted above all with honors. He gave her fine gifts: he assigned to her rights both in the earth and in the barren sea, and the immortal gods honor her greatly. To this day men on earth call on Hecate whenever they wish to make propitiation with the rich sacrificial offerings which the law commands. The man whose prayer is favorably received by the goddess acquires great honor and wealth with ease. Such is the power of Hecate; she has a share in the rights and privileges of every one of the gods born of Earth and Sky.[14]

Even here it is evident that Hecate is not what she once was. Hesiod is at some pains to emphasize her subordination to Zeus, although Zeus treats her always with profound respect:

Nor did the son of Cronus forcibly deprive her of the properties she had received at the hands of the earlier generation of gods, the Titans; she still retains rights on earth and in the sky and on the sea, as assigned in the beginning by the first division of powers.[15]

The tone of the passage suggests a fairly early period of the patriarchalizing process, during which the goddess and her followers must be assured and reassured as to their position in the new order. Indeed, as regards the *Theogony* in general, "The total picture is one of a graduated increase in masculine authority," as Brown observes.[16] From it we may postulate an earlier state of affairs in which Hecate herself was the ruler of earth, sea, and sky. As the patriarchy tightened its hold we imagine her sinking down and down, gaining always in fear and dread what she loses in the attention of the orthodox, until she becomes the accursed outlaw described by Summers.

It will be useful to bear Hecate in mind while considering some of the other great witches of Greek literature, Circe, for example. She turns men to swine, it will be recalled, taking advantage of their appetites; but when Odysseus, warned and armed by Hermes, defeats her plans, she at once yields to him and calls him to her couch. Even then he must be careful, before sleeping with her, to extract from her an oath that she will not unman him.[17]

What Hermes arms Odysseus with is a sacred herb called moly. Exactly what plant Homer intended is not known; Graves thinks it was the wild cyclamen.[18] Other writers have supposed it to be a garlic or onion-shaped plant, which seems to me particularly suggestive, especially since it was given the hero by Hermes Goldenrod, who at an early stage of his mythic development represented the phallus.[19] Odysseus seems to be at least in part another manifestation of the sacred king, subject to many threats, yet able to overcome them and establish his own legitimate rule—the rule of the patriarch.

But the most famous of the Greek witches is Medea, about whom there lingers a real tradition of dread. She is a tremendously complex figure; originally she was apparently either a priestess or even a persona of the Great Mother—the triple goddess. In the famous story of Jason and the Golden Fleece we learn how she was enlisted by the patriarchal adventurers, and made common cause with them against her own people, whom she used with barbaric cruelty—she delayed her father's pursuit of the Greeks by throwing in his path the dismembered limbs of his son, Aetes, her brother. She also contrived the death of Jason's usurping uncle Pelias by her hellish arts, arranging it so that his own children butchered him in an attempt to restore his youth. But this was a secret which she really did possess: from a cauldron filled with ingredients much like those used by the witches in *Macbeth* she brewed an elixir which could restore youth and virility to plants, men, and animals. Jason's own father she restored to youth in this way, although it was necessary to kill him first.

Her patriarchal allies rewarded her for all these services by abandoning her. Jason thought to put her aside when a more advantageous match came up; but she killed the girl along with her own children and then flew off through the air in a chariot drawn by dragons.

I have risked pestering the reader with some details of a story probably already well known to him in order to point out some curious aspects of it. First of all, Medea is connected from the start with Hecate, according to Apollonius Rhodius. Jason, before his liaison with Medea, hears this from her brother Argus: "Haply thou too hast somewhat heard before that one of my sisters useth sorcery by the prompting of Hecate, daughter of Perses.[20] For her part, Medea has already prayed to Hecate that Jason may be spared (a conspiracy of goddesses has prompted Eros to make Medea fall in love with Jason). It is in the temple of Hecate that Jason finds her when he goes to seek her aid, and it is Hecate whom he invokes to help him: "By Hecate herself, by thy parents, and by Zeus, whose hand is over strangers and suppliants, I entreat thee."[21]

The death and rejuvenation of the king is of course right out of Frazer; the fact that the king actually has to die suggests a vigorous early stage of the matriarchy. But the account has been muddied; the later story of Medea's deception of the daughters of Pelias suggests a break-down of the tradition. As for the actual recipe of Medea's hellish brew, we have an excellent account of it in Ovid. Like any stock witch, she invokes Hecate, and then repairs to her cauldron:

Meanwhile the strong potion in the bronze pot is boiling, leaping and frothing white with the swelling foam. In this pot she boils roots cut in a Thessalian vale,[22] together with seeds, flowers, and strong juices. She adds to these ingredients pebbles sought for in the farthest Orient and sands which the ebbing tide of ocean laves.[23] She adds hoar frost gathered under the full moon, the wings of the uncanny screech-owl with the flesh as well, and the entrails of a werewolf which has the power of changing its wild-beast features into a man's. There also in the pot is the scaly skin of a slender Cinyphian water-snake, the liver of a long-lived stag, to which she also adds eggs and the head of a crow nine generations old. When with these and a thousand other nameless things the barbarian woman had prepared her more than mortal plan, she stirred it all up with a branch of the fruitful olive long since dry and well mixed the top and bottom together.[24]

No sixteenth or seventeenth-century European witchfinder would have had any trouble in recognizing Medea as a witch. The picture holds remarkably true across the centuries. Medea was a witch, and a votary of Hecate; more than that, she may originally have been a local variant of Hecate herself. Graves says that she was a Corinthian Demeter.[25] Here in part is his explanation of Demeter:

> Core, Persephone, and Hecate were, clearly, the Goddesses in Triad as Maiden, Nymph, and Crone, at a time when only women practiced the mysteries of agriculture. Core stands for the green corn, Persephone for the ripe ear, and Hecate for the harvested corn—the "carline wife" of the English countryside. But Demeter was the goddess's general title.[26]

Pluto's rape of Persephone "refers to male usurpation of the female agricultural mysteries in primitive times."[27] Thus the continuation of the female-conducted fertility cult, carried out underground by conservative elements, ultimately in an atmosphere of dread and terror. The negative aspects of the cult—sterility, perversion, obstruction—"ligature"—were eventually established in the popular mind. That such a cult did exist is indisputable; what it was in classical times was the Eleusinian Mysteries, which evidently celebrated the disappearance and return of Core. It was strictly a female enterprise; only married women might attend. Herodotus says that these rites were brought to Greece from Egypt,[28] a suggestive detail, as matriarchal ways seemed to have lingered long there, where for example the ruling Pharaoh had ritually to marry his sister because the royal line descended through the woman.

Other Greek cults worthy of notice are the Dionysian Festivals, once again celebrated by women who, in their ecstasy, would rend and tear anyone who came into their hands, even their own children (Euripides, *Bacchae*). Under the Romans this festival became the excuse for indiscriminate brutality, perversion, and disorder. In later chapters we shall have occasion to inquire more closely into the Dionysiac practices of dressing in skins, "raw-eating," and sacrifice.

In these matters, the rites resembled those of Pan who, Graves remarks, "stands for the 'devil' or 'upright man' of the Arcadian fertility cult, which closely resembled the witch-cult of North-western Europe. This man, dressed in a goat-skin, was the chosen lover of the Maenads [the frenzied female worshipers] during their drunken orgies on the high mountains, and sooner or later paid for his privilege with death."²⁹ Arcadia was a byword among the Greeks for rustic simplicity; in this conservative area the worship of the triple goddess would die hard.

Finally we should cite the Orphic Mysteries, in which the death of Orpheus, a sacred king torn to pieces by Maenads, was ritually reenacted at specified intervals, long after the Greek city-states had been thoroughly subdued by the Patriarchal invaders. These survivals should remind us of the toughness and longevity of the old ways, and their resistance to man's logical and humane provisions. "I expect that Woman will be the last thing civilized by Man," as George Meredith puts it.³⁰

The genius of Euripides altered the Medea legend significantly; with him she becomes an archetypal savage war-bride. It is a magnificent achievement, but one often at odds with the earlier material. Euripides may even have been rewarded by the city of Corinth, as Graves reports, for having blackened Medea's reputation by putting all the blame for the murder of her children upon her, thus refuting an earlier story implicating the city.³¹

Among modern literary treatments of Medea and the triple-goddess in her various manifestations, the best are surely Mary Renault's, particularly *The Bull from the Sea* (1952) and *The King*

Must Die (1958). She re-creates convincingly the atmosphere of surviving awe of the great Mother through which the early Greek chieftains must have picked their way. And the student should not neglect Graves's own salute to the Mother in her more benign aspect as muse, *The White Goddess* (1948).[32]

The Romans were for the most part content to build upon the Greek myths, as in the case of Ovid's graceful elaborations, quoted above; but they did bring elements of their own to what has become known as the Graeco-Roman pantheon. Prominent among these were relics of the Etruscans, their mysterious long-term rivals in Italy, finally superceded by them. The Etruscan religion is said to have been rich in superstition. Then in the time of her fatness Rome was host to every Eastern god and cult imaginable; fashion, wealth, and boredom made her a great patroness of religions. Many of these were of distinctly matriarchal origin: the popular cult of Isis, for example, brought from Egypt and first recognized under Caligula; Cybele, the great Phrygian Aphrodite whose worship required the self-castration of her priests (in memory of the death of her lover Attis, a sacred king); and *Bona Dea*—the good goddess—whose rites, again carried on entirely by women, were grossly sexual according to Juvenal. He accused the worshipers of satisfying their lust with any man who came along, however lowborn or old:

> The secrets of the Goddess named the Good,
> Are ev'n by Boys and Barbers understood:
> Where the rank Matrons, dancing to the Pipe,
> Gig with their Bums, and for Action ripe,
> With Musick rais'd, they spread abroad their Hair;
> And toss their Heads like an enamour'd Mare.[33]

Of particular interest to our study are the Roman myths of the underworld. These were of such a grim picturesque intensity as to have made themselves remembered in Western civilization until this very day; witchcraft scholarship gives them a large part of the credit for some of the wilder details of Christian demonology. And almost all of this material came from the supplanted Etruscan ritual:

It was above all from primitive Etruria that the Romans borrowed their conception of the infernal regions and its *[sic]* inhabitants. In the Etruscan underworld the naive and terrifying visions common to all primitive religions mingle with abstract conceptions of more developed systems.[34]

The Roman underworld was inhabited by such creatures as Tuchulcha, "a female demon with ferocious eyes, the ears of an ass, a beak in place of a mouth, two serpents turned around her head and a third around her arm."[35] She was entirely the sort of being familiar to the desert saints, as well as to sixteenth-century German painters.

Among the Roman authors who give special attention to witchcraft and sorcery, Pliny (the Elder) must not be omitted. Summers calls his *Natural History* "a regular storehouse of charms and magic recipes."[36] It has been published in a splendid Centaur edition, courtesy of Southern Illinois University Press. But the most interesting of these writers are surely the novelists, if we may call them so, Lucius Apuleius and Gaius Petronius, called Arbiter. Apuleius's famous story, *The Golden Ass*, is founded upon the transformation of a young man by witchcraft into an ass. It is a book in which needy young fellows hire themselves out to guard the newly dead from the profanations of witches, who "are in the habit of gnawing bits of flesh off dead men's faces for use in their magical concoctions."[37] The witch Pamphile smears herself with flying ointment and tears off through the air. The hero tries to do the same, gets the wrong ointment, and finds himself an ass indeed, in which guise he has many adventures. The whole novel is a treasury of supernatural lore.

At Trimalchio's banquet, which forms the central episode of Petronius's *Satyricon*, stories are told. Two in particular are of interest here. The first is told by an ex-slave named Niceros who says that he once went out late on a moonlit night with a soldier. As they were walking along where the road runs among tombstones, he was horrified to find his companion change himself into a wolf, give a doleful howl and lope off into the woods. The werewolf later broke into a sheepfold and was driven off wounded; sure enough the soldier next day had a gash in his neck.

The host caps that one with a grisly tale of witches come after the corpse of a child. A brave servant rushes out to the defense, but is horribly mutilated; meanwhile the witches carry off the little body, for their rites, leaving a changeling of straw in its place. These stories are intended to be taken as true, and are accepted as such by the guests, whose merriment as a consequence undergoes a considerable chill.[38]

The ancient world presents a concept of witchcraft complete in every detail, essentially undifferentiated from that of the great witchcraft delusion and attendant persecutions of the sixteenth and seventeenth centuries in Europe. It is reinforced at every point by the Bible and by Judeo-Christian religious thought. As late as A.D. 900, witchcraft, not yet an organized heresy, was thought of by the Church in classical, as well as biblical, terms. The *Canon Episcopi* (ca. 900), a key document in the study of witchcraft, as famous for its mildness and good sense as the later "enlightened" laws are notorious for cruelty and hysteria, has this notable passage:

> It is also not to be omitted that certain abandoned women perverted by Satan, seduced by illusions and phantasms of demons, believe and openly profess that, in the dead of night, they ride upon certain beasts with the pagan goddess Diana, with a countless horde of women, and in the silence of the dead of night fly over vast tracts of country, and obey her commands as their mistress, while they are summoned to her service on other nights.[39]

There are Satan and Diana side by side, in the very teeth of the Church's displeasure, at the end of the first millennium. And do not forget that Diana, or Artemis, is the earthly name of the triple goddess, still potent, still fearful, still very much to be reckoned with by men.

4. Development of the Orthodox Position

 Already in the *Canon Episcopi* we find the seeds of conspiracy. True, the *Canon*, with great good sense, makes no doubt of the fact that the witches are deluded by Satan. Their nocturnal meetings, their flights through the air, all their "trips," are hallucinations. Nevertheless the material was there for later authorities to interpret in their own way: what if all these gatherings and entertainments were not illusory?

The orthodox case against the witches is essentially a dual one: first, that witches by their devices hurt people, animals, and crops, particularly by promoting sickness, sterility, and storms. Any witchcraft trial will present dozens, sometimes hundreds of items in evidence of this contention. These acts of harm, properly called *maleficia*, are the source of the village hostility toward the witch, who acts as a lightning rod for rural discontent during times of poverty, sickness, or natural calamity.

But officialdom, both clerical and lay, began to identify a second basic kind of offense in witches, which was even more heinous and in the long run much more harmful: heresy. A witch might behave toward her neighbors with exemplary propriety, yet if she took part in nocturnal assemblies convened to blaspheme against God, Jesus, Mary, and the saints, and to venerate Satan and his angels, then she was ten times worse than an old woman who, in a fit of pique, killed somebody's sow. It was the authorities who pushed this kind of inquiry, not the ordinary people (who were much more concerned with sows); by the time of the great persecutions, charges of heresy had prevailed over charges of *maleficia,* and had become the important issues at the trials. By the seventeenth century, an old woman accused of killing a sow would typically find herself faced with a stock list of questions about attending a *sabbat* and worshiping a goat-like god.

Both sorts of charges are to be found in classical and biblical traditions. The Greek and Roman witches were understood to be organized, to a certain extent, but their rites, while held in horror and detestation, were not absolutely removed from the state religion. Hecate was a goddess who had a place in the pantheon; a dread being, she could nevertheless be placated and propitiated by gifts and prayer. The idea of witchcraft as an uncompromising, implacably hostile system seems more likely to have grown up from the Judeo-Christian side; and yet we know that the early Church compromised again and again with prestigious pagan divinities.

There are at present two major theories which seek to explain witchcraft's evolution into a Christian heresy—and hence, its suffering during the sixteenth and seventeenth-century persecutions. The first is a fundamental tenet of what we may call the skeptical position. Here it is expounded by one of its leading proponents, Rossell Hope Robbins:

> Probably the chief reason why sorcery was turned into heresy was the success of the inquisitors in obliterating previous heresies. All through the thirteenth century, the Inquisition had concentrated its forces on the inhabitants of southern France, and with the work of the notorious inquisitor, Bernardus Guidonis, from 1308 to 1323, the Albigensians and other heretics had been exterminated. About 1320, says the *Encyclopedia Britannica* (11th ed.), "the persecution stopped for lack of an object." Witchcraft was in fact *invented* to fill the gap; the first trials for sorcery were held in Provence.[1] Between 1350 and 1400 various trials allowed the Dominican inquisitors to think out a theory of sorcery as treason against God.[2]

The skeptical position, focusing as it does upon man's boundless capacity to deceive himself, and better, to enrich himself by gathering the fruits of his self-deception from his weaker neighbors, is always, it seems to me, a strong one. Thus Robbins continues: "Everyone throughout Europe was a potential witch, a potential heretic, and therefore a potential source of income to the inquisitors, who shared with the civil authorities the confiscated properties of all those they considered as heretics."[3]

Robbins and his fellow skeptics always point to the possibilities of *gain* from witchcraft, which were enormous; to psychological aberrations, old family and clan hatreds, rivalries in towns, greedy and corrupt churchmen, venal lawyers, credulous mobs and irritable, crack-brained old women. Without doubt a considerable percentage—perhaps up to 90 percent—of witchcraft phenomena is due to these and similar causes. Yet one may still question the premise that the Church deliberately formulated a new heresy to replace the ones which it had extinguished. We shall leave rebuttal however for the moment to consider the second major theory of the development of the witchcraft heresy in the fourteenth century, and that is the anthropological one. No one is better qualified to state it than Margaret Murray herself:

> In the thirteenth century the Church opened its long-drawn-out conflict with Paganism in Europe by declaring "witchcraft" to be a "sect" and heretical. It was not till the fourteenth century that the two religions came to grips. . . . The fifteenth century marks the first great victories of the Church. Beginning with the trials in Lorraine in 1408 the Church moved triumphantly against Joan of Arc and her followers in 1431, against Gilles de Rais and his coven in 1440, against the witches of Brescia in 1457. Towards the end of the century the Christian power was so well established that the Church felt that the time had come for an organized attack, and in 1484 Pope Innocent VIII published his Bull against "witches." All through the sixteenth and seventeenth centuries the battle raged. The Pagans fought a gallant, though losing, fight against a remorseless and unscrupulous enemy; every inch of the field was disputed.[4]

So here it seems that the fourteenth century was when battle was joined, because Christianity did not feel itself strong enough to try the issue until then. Margaret Murray speaks confidently of a struggle between two powers, two religions, almost equal at the outset. Notice also the passing reference to Gilles de Rais as a cult leader, a theory which is by no means widely held among scholars.

I have wished to take up these arguments together because both of them, it seems to me, are liable to the same basic objection. Both speak of the Church as a completely coherent force, as careful and as well in order as a good chess player. Yet surely this was not the case. Quite to the contrary, the Church in the fourteenth century, torn by dissension and schism, was at the brink of the major upheaval which we call the Reformation. It is perhaps this unsettled, fragmented state of the church that we must identify as the motive force behind the persecutions, and not any well-conceived plan.[5]

To be sure powerful individual voices were to be heard, loud against witchcraft, in this period—Popes, jurists, politicians—and we shall need to consider some of their charges in this chapter. Some of them surely were strong enough to set in motion large forces of church and state. Yet a number of other considerations must be weighed. The geography of the persecutions, for instance, is most significant. All authorities agree that the worst excesses were to be found in—Rome, where the Pope's control was strongest? Spain, where the Church's zeal was at its height? No, Germany, the very battlefield of the Reformation, where no doctrine was secure and no security was certain.

There where Catholics and Protestants vied with each other in bloodthirstiness, hundreds of thousands went to the flames. Surely the unsettled times must bear a major share of the blame. It is worth remarking that England, which has one of the *best* records in Europe in witchcraft persecution, was also fortunate enough to escape the continental excesses in religious turmoil, thanks to the Elizabethan compromise. It is instructive to note the periods when English persecution, such as it was, was at its worst: invariably they coincided with periods of deep anxiety, such as the end of Elizabeth's reign, or the reign of Charles I. Worst of all—the brief and ugly rule of the witchfinder Matthew Hopkins—is the summer of 1645, just after Naseby, when political and social confusion were at their height.

On the other hand, it is significant to find that Spain has an unusually good record in dealing with witchcraft. Her practical inquisitors, so quick to detect any vestige of Protantism, brushed aside charges of witchcraft to concentrate upon weightier matters. They could afford to do so because of the solidity of their position. It was precisely where the Church was *not* secure that the persecutions raged hottest: Germany, France, and Scotland, oddly enough, which is often cited as second only to Germany in severity. But here again we see a powerful religious upheaval, the one in which England was able to put off until the mid-seventeenth century: a Catholic queen banished, a powerful Protestant regency, a country divided into progressive Protestant lowlands and conservative Catholic highlands.[6]

For the historian of the orthodox party, the fourteenth-century shift in emphasis to heresy is a simple matter. It was then, Summers tells us, that sorcery was "violently unmasked" as heresy, "and the whole horrid craft then first authoritatively exposed in its darkest colours and most abominable manifestations, as had indeed existed from the first, but had been carefully hidden and scrupulously concealed."[7]

"The first Papal Bull directly launched against the black art and its professors," according to Summers, "was that of Alexander IV, 13 December, 1258, addressed to the Franciscan inquisitors." Lea, working from a list prepared by the German scholar Joseph Hansen, supports this judgment. The first important bull, however, is that of John XXII, February 27, 1318. This Pope Summers calls "a man of serious character, of austere and simple habits, broadly cultivated" (he is quoting an earlier author).[9] John XXII also seems to have been a paranoid. Robbins calls him "One of the most superstitious of all popes, always imagining his enemies were plotting to take his life by sorcery."[10]

John XXII, born Jacques d'Euse, was an Avignon pope. He does not seem to have been noteworthy for beauty of character, Summers notwithstanding. There is general agreement, however, that he is the first pope to have promulgated important doctrine on witchcraft. He was "the first to promote the theory of witchcraft and spread obscurantism," Robbins says.[11] Lea gives details of six major pronouncements from him on the subject of sorcery and witchcraft, 1318, February 27; 1320, August 22; 1326 or 27; 1327, November 8; 1330, November 4; and 1331, April 12.[12] Among the details of these bulls given by Lea are many significant touches.

John accuses members of his own court of divination and sorcery by means of mirrors, rings, and images; sometimes they wickedly use "Dianae," which Lea takes to be succubi. The classical tradition at the intrigue-ridden court of Avignon! In fairness to the pope, it must be said that there very well may have been plots against him; the atmosphere was conducive to them. Summers fully acquiesces in John's charges, and gives all the horrid details: "Two men had been arrested at the gates of Avignon, and in their luggage was found poisons, noxious herbs, arsenic, quicksilver, dried toads, lizards, the tails of rats, spiders, the hair of a hanged malefactor, vervain, marjoram, mint, and many other compounds for philtres, and above all wax figures of the Pope, cunningly hidden among the crumb of large loaves."[13] Personally I find these details no harder to believe than many others which are better attested, those of the Chambre Ardente affair of late seventeenth-century Paris, for example, where an international ring of poisoners was broken up. Summers's credulity and fixity of belief, however, are not likely to win much support for himself or his causes; in the paragraphs before the one I have quoted, he relates with equal seriousness, and satisfaction, the massacre of a group of lepers, Jews, and sorcerers who were accused in 1321 of a plot to poison all the wells of France.

It may be said then that the personal character of a pope influenced the spread of witchcraft doctrine; but it must also be remembered that the captivity was a time of desperation in the Church, when Rome was sunk in lethargy and ruin, and the papacy itself on the edge of the Great Schism. By the time of John's bull of 1318, Lea notes, "the heretical character of sorcery is assumed fully."[14] John did not decide that sorcerers were heretics; it was a doctrine that had been growing slowly along with the mediaeval Church itself, as it pursued its exceedingly tortuous way through thickets of theology and politics. The great bloodbath which these early decisions helped to bring about did not come until Christianity was actively at war with itself across a wide front.

But before the bulls against witchcraft, there were bulls against heresy. The curious fact is that they very much resemble the later ones against witchcraft. This is of course a vital part of the skeptical case against the Church; when it had exterminated the Cathars, for example, it merely turned to another group, using the same data, the same accusations. It will be necessary to go back a minute to these earlier documents.

The Cathars, Catharites, or Catharists, were members of a loosely defined, widespread heresy, prominent in Europe from the tenth to the fourteenth centuries. Among their other detestable doctrines was that central one propounded by Mani, the dualism of Good and Evil. Like the Manichees and the Yezidees, the Cathars recognized Satan as the God of this world, although they did not for that reason venerate him. On the contrary, they professed themselves ardent followers of Christ. Their doctrinal peculiarities however made them odious to the Church, which in its wrath abused them in the most extravagant manner. The famous Albigensians were a branch of the Cathars. These were brutally stamped out by a series of thirteenth-century crusades. Their extermination was in fact just completed by the reign of John XXII—hence the conclusions of the skeptics.

Now the Cathars, and the Albigensians, were widely accused of a whole catalogue of depravities, particularly these, which will be familiar to the student of witchcraft: flying through the air to nocturnal meetings by the aid of demons, horrid sexual orgies and perversions, worship of devils, child murder, preparation of potions from all sorts of abhorrent materials, blasphemy and foul abuse of God. These details, gathered from popular superstitions and folk tales, were certainly convenient for the Church in its procedures, but we must not make the mistake of thinking that it used them in any cynical spirit. Quite the contrary: as Lea puts it, speaking of an important bull against these heretics, by Gregory IX, "he can scarce find words to express his grief and horror."[15] The text is worthy of being printed here:

> The whole church weeps and groans and can find no
> consolation when such things are wrought in its bosom. It is
> the most detestable of heresies, a horror to those who hear
> of it; opposed to reason, contrary to piety, hateful to all
> hearts, inimical to earth and heaven, against which the very
> elements should arise. It would not be sufficient punishment
> if the whole earth rose against them, if the very stars
> revealed their iniquities to the whole world, so that not only

men but the elements themselves should combine for their destruction and sweep them from the face of the earth, without sparing age or sex, so that they should be in eternal opprobrium to the nations.[16]

There is no doubting the sincerity of this outburst, or so it seems to me. The orthodox position on the matter is very plain and indeed logical, granting its major premise: The Catharist heresies and the witchcraft heresy *were* connected; both were devices of Satan in his never-ending war against the Church. When the first failed, he turned to the second. We miss the point, I think, if we imagine a cold-blooded decision on the part of the hierarchy to turn its inquisitorial apparatus to new profits, upon the extinction of old ones.[17]

The skeptics are probably right to an extent. Having grown so great as to be hedged round with enemies, the Church developed organs to deal with them, only to find that the organs continued to produce enemies to deal with—the well-known self-perpetuating bureaucracy. The argument may however be carried too far.

Among papal writings against witchcraft, the student should be aware of the following: after those of John XXII, there are a number of publications by his successor Benedict XII, who was also zealous against sorcerers. Gregory XI has one, Alexander V has one; there is one by Martin V, and no less than four from Eugenius IV. The second of these (1437) is of particular interest as a catalogue of offenses, particularly of *maleficia* (the sabbat is not mentioned). Succeedings popes who acted against witchcraft were Nicholas V, Callixtus III, Pius II, and Sixtus IV, whose vigorous pronouncements against the Waldensian heretics greatly aided the process of mingling sorcery and heresy in the popular mind.

These brief references are all by way of building up to the greatest of all papal utterances on the subject of witchcraft, Innocent VIII's *Summis desiderantes affectibus* (December 5, 1484). This bull has over the years become so notorious that one sometimes hears it mentioned as a "unique" or "extraordinary" document, as Summers indignantly puts it.[18] In truth it is one of the key texts in witchcraft studies, but it is best viewed as the culmination of generations of papal concern.

Innocent VIII (1432-92), born Giovanni Battista Cibo, was a Genoese, an aristocrat, and a scholar. He was also a formidable opponent of all heterodoxy; among his many accomplishments against it are his crusades against the Waldensians, his attack on the Hussites, and his persecution of Pico Della Mirandola ("an eminently proper precaution," says Summers).[19] His bull of 1484 is a landmark for several reasons: first, because of its widespread, wholesale condemnation of the heresy of witchcraft over a large territory (earlier bulls usually dealt with one case, or one area); second, because it rebuked both laity and clergy for their interference with the work of the inquisition,[20] and was therefore triumphantly used by this body, in particular the Dominicans Henry Kramer and James Sprenger[21] as their sword and shield—specifically it served as introduction to their notorious *Malleus Maleficarum*, handbook of the witchfinders. Third, because it was reprinted with each edition of this much-reprinted book (and because printing was at the time making its first great impression on European culture), it became far better known than any earlier pronouncement about witchcraft.

Summis desiderantes affectibus is one of the few early witchcraft documents readily obtainable today, and should be consulted by every student. It is not long; it may be found in its entirety prefixed to the *Malleus*, which is in print; in Summers's *Geography of Witchcraft*, and in Robbins's *Encyclopedia of Witchcraft and Demonology*. What it says, in effect, is this: the Church proclaims and reaffirms the absolute necessity to extirpate all heresy. Such heresy, namely witchcraft (and the classic offenses against increase, piety, and good order are named) is rampart throughout Germany, yet some officious people, denying the fact, have hindered the inquisitors Kramer and Sprenger in their inquiries into these crimes. Such people are enjoined to cease their interference, on pain of their own excommunication and "yet more terrible penalties." And furthermore all the facilities of the Faith are to be made available to them for their work. If any man "rashly oppose this page," "let him know that on him will fall the wrath of God Almighty and the blessed Apostles Peter and Paul."

This bull set the stage for the final phase of the persecutions. As

Margaret Murray says, it "let loose the full force of the Church."[22] It "rang the tocsin," says Scott, "and set forth in most dismal colours the guilt, while it stimulated the inquisitors to the most unsparing discharge of their duty in searching out and punishing the guilty."[23] And these inquisitors, Kramer and Sprenger, produced the definitive text for the witchfinders, *Malleus Maleficarum*, 1486, "The Hammer of the witches." This document, which may be called the fruit of the Church's labors over several centuries in the field of witchcraft, must now be examined.

There were papal bulls after 1484, many, and some of them important, but none more significant than Innocent's; and there were treatises on witchcraft after the *Malleus*, but none more crucial to the orthodox position. Here is set down definitively what witches are, what they do, how they may be apprehended, brought to justice, tortured and executed. The book is a veritable primer, and was used as such all over Europe. Moreover it provided the model, and in most cases, the basis, for all the witchcraft texts which followed it. It is the principal statement of the orthodox position.

Both Kramer and Sprenger were Dominicans, and organization men of genius. Their careers are similar; each showed promise at an early age, and each was astute enough to attach himself to the right people, Kramer to the archbishop of Salzburg, and Sprenger to the officials of the order, eventually the Master General, Fra Salvo Cassetta. Each was noteworthy for crusading zeal, and strict adherence to orthodoxy: Kramer was a great defender of Papal supremacy, and a major persecutor of Waldensians and Picards as well as witches; Sprenger was first Inquisitor Extraordinary and later Provincial of the whole German Province, and a champion of the Confraternity of the Most Holy Rosary. Between them they produced the book which Summers proclaims "the ultimate, irrefutable, unarguable authority."[24]

The text is divided into three parts. The first is mostly philosophical; its first question asks "Whether the belief that there are such beings as witches is so essential a part of the Catholic Faith that obstinacy to maintain the opposite opinion manifestly savours of heresy." The answer is, it is, and it does. A long disquisition follows, under many headings, of the powers given to devils and to witches to do harm. Included are certain more practical matters relating to the incubus and succubus, as well as the query, why is it that women are chiefly addicted to evil superstitions? Their feebler capacity is adduced, as well as their debased history ("The first temptress, Eve, and her imitators") and lower nature. All this is "indicated," say the inquisitors, "by the etymology of the word; for *Femina* comes from *Fe* and *Minus*"[25]—less faith. No section of the book gives a clearer indication of the temper of its authors.

The second part of the *Malleus*, however, is that which I especially wish to consider here, because it deals with the actual crimes of witches as they were now codified, at the end of the fifteenth century. The section is divided into sixteen chapters "treating of the methods by which the works of witchcraft are wrought and directed," followed by eight chapters devoted to "how they may be successfully annulled and dissolved." The chapter headings will, I think, serve to indicate the nature of the material.

1. Of the several methods by which devils through witches entice and allure the innocent to the increase of that horrid craft and company
2. Of the way whereby a formal pact with Evil is made
3. How they are transported from place to place
4. Here follows the way whereby witches copulate with those devils known as Incubi
5. Witches commonly perform their spells through the sacraments of the Church. And how they impair the powers of generation, and how they may cause other ills to happen to God's creatures of all kinds. But herein we except the question of the influence of the stars
6. How witches impede and prevent the Power of Procreation
7. How, as it were, they deprive man of his virile member
8. Of the manner whereby they change men into the shapes of beasts
9. How devils may enter the human body and the head without doing any hurt, when they cause such metamorphosis by means of prestidigitation
10. Of the method by which devils through the operations of

witches sometimes actually possess men

11. Of the method by which they can inflict every sort of infirmity, generally ills of the graver kind
12. Of the way how in particular they afflict men with other like infirmities
13. How witch midwives commit most horrid crimes when they either kill children or offer them to devils in most accursed wise
14. Here followeth how witches injure cattle in various ways
15. How they raise and stir up hailstorms and tempests, and cause lightning to blast both men and beasts
16. Of three ways in which men and not women may be discovered to be addicted to witchcraft: divided into three heads: and first of the witchcraft of archers.

At this point the inquisitors move to the subject of remedies. Let us however pause to gloss some of these articles. First, there should be observed in them an expert wedding of ordinary barnyard *maleficia*—a whole chapter on injuries to cattle—and the darker crimes of heresy. Note too that the heretical element has now taken full precedence: we begin by considering the "formal pact with Evil." What all this amounts to is *not* hysteria, but quite the contrary: the application to witchcraft of formal logic and scholarship. That is the horror of it. The great achievements of Western man in disciplined thinking, here applied to all sorts of vague, repressed fears, have indeed produced monsters.

The strong sexual aspect of many of these items is evident; there are several theories to explain it. At the moment it is enough to quote the orthodox principle involved, which is propounded with perfect clarity in section 1 of the *Malleus:* "All witchcraft comes from carnal lust, which is in women insatiable."[26] The pursuit of this line leads the inquisitors into some strange episodes, which we might hope to interpret as some sort of monkish humor; but they are probably to be taken in all seriousness. Thus this anecdote, much ridiculed by Reginald Scot:

And what, then, is to be thought of those witches who in this way sometimes collect male organs in great numbers, as

many as twenty or thirty members together, and put them
in a bird's nest . . . . ? For a certain man tells that, when he
had lost his member, he approached a known witch to ask
her to restore it to him. She told the afflicted man to climb
a certain tree, and that he might take which he liked out of
a nest in which there were several members. And when he
tried to take a big one, the witch said: "you must not take
that one;" adding "because it belonged to a parish priest."[27]

This would seem to be a classic case of the authorities victimized by
a dirty joke. One need only change the ending to "our parish
priest."

Chapter 5 is interesting in that it formalizes the concept that the
witches' rites are performed in blasphemous imitation of Christian
ritual, which is one of Montague Summers's strongest points of
rebuttal against the anthropologist Margaret Murray. Chapters 9
and 10 deal with the question of possession, which played an
important role in the trials. Chapter 13 is a further indication of the
pervasive misogyny of the work and indeed many of the works of
the Church at the time. Midwives came in for more than their share
of opprobrium, because of 1) their officious intermediacy in the
mysteries of birth, and the superstitious fear, and perhaps jealousy,
which this whole process inspired in men; 2) the high infant
mortality, for which they were handy scapegoats; and 3) the
likelihood that a midwife was a "cunning woman," who might
know other arts as well. Accusation of child-murder is an old
symptom of hysteria; the charge has been laid to every minority
group or common enemy at one time or another, notably the Jews,
the Cathars, the witches, the Moslems, and the Germans in World
War I. (Accusations of this kind against the Nazis seem all too well-
founded.)

As to the last item, "The witchcraft of archers," this is a curious
survival of a long-standing prejudice against archers, as using a
new-fangled and uncanny weapon, which can kill at a distance.
This antipathy is very old; evidences of it may be found in the *Iliad*,
where Paris, by no means the most glorious in arms among the
combatants, is represented as an archer. Here there is perpetuated
the belief that certain "wizards" shoot at the cross on Good Friday,

thereby procuring magical powers for their arrows, which they then turn against their enemies. "Oh the cruelty and injury to the Saviour!"[28]

Part three of the *Malleus* deals with judicial procedure. This horrible document, furnished with exact details, set the standard throughout Europe; as Summers boasts, it "lay on the bench of every judge, on the desk of every magistrate."[29] Its various chapters prescribe the proper number of witnesses to be called, their examination, the interrogation of suspects, with a full account of torture, shaving, searching for devil's marks; conduct of the trial, methods of sentencing, the judgments appropriate to the several kinds of malefactors—and finally the proper forms for handling the condemned to the flames: ". . . we have exerted our utmost endeavor by various fitting methods to convert you to salvation; but you have been given up to your sin and led away and seduced by an evil spirit, and have chosen to be tortured with fearful and eternal torment in hell, and that your temporal body should here be consumed in the flames."[30]

It is all so damnably logical, and the logic is attended with small pity. To be sure, the inquisitors recommend, in the case of "one taken and convicted, but denying everything" (question 31), that if he finally relent and confess his guilt, even at the place of execution, that he be received as "a penitant heretic," and merely be imprisoned for life. "Nevertheless," they add, "the Judges ought not to place much faith in a conversion of this sort; and furthermore, they can always punish him on account of the temporal injuries which he has committed" (p. 261). O the cruelty to the Savior! The chief objection to the orthodox position is not that it was founded upon hysteria, suspicion, repressed guilt or panic fear, as we may say of many little village persecutions; it is that it covered these all too human frailties with a logical, systematic, procedural armor of triple proof, so that it ended by persuading itself, and almost everyone else, that torture and murder were the only reasonable responses to its anxieties.

5. The Triumph of Orthodoxy: Laws, Texts, Trials

With the *Malleus Maleficarum,* the stage is set for the great persecutions of the sixteenth and seventeenth centuries—the High Renaissance, note, not the "Middle Ages" so often associated with witch-hunting. The great trials were a feature of a more enlightened age; as Goya observed, *"El sueno de la razon produce monstruos"* (The dream of reason produces monsters).[1] In the twentieth century we too have known the darker face of human progress.

It seems clear that the break-up of mediaeval institutions and mediaeval certainties contributed to the subsequent broils and torments. It has *seemed* clear that the witch persecutions were an organic development from earlier heretic persecutions, and we have noted several theories advanced to explain the process. Recent scholarship, however, has identified several key transitional trial records as forgeries. The honor for this discovery must go to Norman Cohn *(Europe's Inner Demons,* 1975), although Richard Kieckhefer, working independently *(European Witch Trials,* 1976), reached the same conclusions at almost the same time.

Witchcraft historians have pointed to "the immediate consequences" of the great heresy trials: the 1275 burning of Angele de la Barthe, cited by Robbins as "the first person executed for witchcraft" *(Encyclopedia, p.* 208); the first mass trial and execution, in Toulouse, 1335; the trials at Toulouse and Carcassonne, by 1350; the trial and execution of a woman in Orta,

Italy, during the 1340's; and an execution in Como in 1360: all these never happened, as Cohn can prove. Evidence for them rests on "three fabrications, dating respectively from the fifteenth, sixteenth, and nineteenth centuries."[2]

The exposure of the Toulouse and Carcassonne trials is particularly telling; it was here that the inquisitors were supposed to have melded standard charges of *maleficia* with distorted Catharist doctrine to form the first witch-hunt. All of it, however, now appears as the fantasy of a nineteenth-century romanticizer and hoaxer, Lamothe-Langon.

What are the consequences of these revelations? For one thing, the development from heresy persecution to witchcraft persecution is not as simple and straightforward as it has heretofore appeared. The witch trials probably *were* developed from earlier heresy trials, but not in the smooth, self-assured manner which some historians have ascribed to the Church. Furthermore, the emphasis in such development now shifts from France to Italy, a more logical area for it, according to Kieckhefer.[3]

Advances, if they may be called so, in the law must now occupy our attention. Witchcraft, like all the fine arts, passed at a certain point in its development from the clergy to the laity. Many of the choicest excesses of the persecutions were carried out by the civil authorities. Following the Church's lead, the nations passed laws against witchcraft which eventually led to its being considered a state crime as well as a heresy.

From the earliest times, governments have proceeded against heterodoxy; we have seen King Saul embarrassed at having to break his own codes. The name usually given to traffic with false gods is *sorcery*. Contemporary scholars are particularly fond of ingenious demonstrations that sorcery and witchcraft are two different phenomena; but the impression persists that in the popular mind they have always been indistinguishable. Thus Robbins: "Witchcraft, then, differed from sorcery in that it was a form of religion, a Christian heresy. Witchcraft was restricted to a few countries of Western Europe. . . . Witchcraft was a part of religion; sorcery part of folklore."[4]

This is a sound, but extremely limited, definition of witchcraft. Africans have their own name for witches, as we have noted; so do Chinese and Brazilians. True, witchcraft may be viewed as an exclusively Christian heresy; but why force one's inquiries into such a narrow channel? Many useful insights into European witchcraft phenomena may be adduced from studies of the *brujos* of the Amazon Basin, for example (see ch. 8 below).

More important still, however nice the scholars may be in their definitions, popular accounts, which are in many cases the sources for these definitions, are vague in the extreme. The witches in the Grimm material, for example, are simply cannibal monsters, much like the Jews in Chaucer, or Marlowe. Shakespeare's "witches" are in some cases obviously sorcerers (*2 Henry VI*, 1, 4), and in others agencies of fate (*Macbeth*), but they are called "witches" nonetheless: the audience demanded it. "Witchcraft" is a term of opprobrium both wide and deep; he who would sound it to the bottom would do well to follow Kieckhefer, who uses it "in an inclusive sense," for "sortilegus," "maleficus," "veneficus," "striga," and so forth.[5]

To do so is not to ignore changing usage of the term. The early codes did not of course conceive of witchcraft activity, however they called it, as the vast conspiracy known to later jurists. Yet the people they warned against would have been recognizable at any time as "witches." The revised Salic law, published 751-64, guards against false accusations of cannibalistic witchcraft; and the synod of Tours in 813 warns against all magic as a snare of the Devil; the synod of Paris, 829, prescribes severe punishment for Satan's followers.

"The earlier Middle Ages were relatively lenient toward heresy and sorcery," Jeffrey Russell tells us.[6] The gradual mustering of laws to match new definitions of witchcraft is a long story. By the time of the great persecutions, fierce codes were in effect, like the so-called Carolina Code of 1532, which governed witchcraft trials throughout the Holy Roman Empire, and the English statutes, Henry VIII's of 1542, Elizabeth's of 1563 and James's of 1604. Even harsher than these laws, however, were the special commissions which in many cases superceded them. "These commissions," Robbins comments, "were the bane of Scottish law."[7] They were not only numerous but powerful, having in many cases the right not only to investigate, but to judge and pronounce sentence, even to death.

France, so often racked by heresies, crusades, and inquisitions, also presents a murky legal picture during the witch craze. The Salic law was clear enough, and like others of its time, remarkable for temperance and good sense: it demanded physical proof of a definite evil act. Moreover, anyone defaming another as a witch without sufficient proof had to pay damages. These wise provisions were gradually chipped away by the force of various Church rulings, in particular those formulated by the University of Paris. There was not, as far as I can make out, a definitive French royal pronouncement on witchcraft as a heresy (though many on witchcraft as sorcery) until Louis XIV's Edict of 1682, which put a stop to the persecutions. This move was forced upon the king by the sensational revelations of the Burning Court (Chambre Ardente Affair), which threatened to implicate almost everyone connected with the throne. Louis found a good reason to bring the witch finding to a halt when it reached his former mistress, Madame de Montespan.

This murkiness was the worst aspect of witchcraft's legal character. Even the Carolina Code, a harsh law, was eventually *appealed to* by convicted witches in the Empire, because of their sufferings at the hands of courts which, at their own whims, far exceeded it. In England, too, the judges had wide latitude: if Sir Matthew Hale had not admitted spectral evidence, for example, at the Bury St. Edmunds trials in 1645, the accused might have got off. But once this sort of evidence was allowed, no alibi was possible, because though you could prove that you had been a hundred miles from the scene of a crime, this was only physical evidence; your spectre, or spirit, might at the same time have been observed committing the crime in question. Those familiar with Salem will recognize the fatal logic involved. There, in conscious imitation of the Bury St. Edmunds proceedings, the court also allowed this sort of evidence, to the utter destruction of good procedure or good sense. It should also be remembered that the Salem trials were conducted by a specially constituted court, against the irregularity of which there was a certain amount of protest, even at the time. One defendant, Giles Corey, seems to have refused to plead on these grounds, and was consequently pressed to death. (This was not as a punishment for witchcraft, nor as torture to get him to confess, but simply as a means to induce him to plead, because as the law then stood, if a man did not plead, he could not be tried.)

Salem, like many other places, departed from ordinary legal procedure at many points, for which it later confessed itself guilty, and did public penance, which is more than happened in Europe, where children also figured prominently as witnesses; where hysterical, mentally deficient, and even totally insane people were heard with great attention from the witness box, and where court officials looted defendants' homes while the trials were still in progress. The conclusion to be drawn is that statutes were not so much to blame; it was the mass departure from government by law which was the cause of many of the worst effects of the witch-hunts.

Many of the classical authorities on witchcraft were jurists, who then as now sometimes thought to crown a legal career by writing a book. From their ranks, and from those of the inquisitors and other church officials, came practically all of the great orthodox texts. Here is a list of some of the more important writers of the great age of witchcraft—from, say, 1450 to 1700—and their books. Some of these have been republished, mostly by the indefatigable Summers, and all are quoted extensively by him and other encyclopedists such as Robbins and Lea. A Dutch firm, Theatrum Orbis Terrarum Ltd., has been engaged in bringing out a series called Bibliotheca Diabolica, which will presumably make all of them available in reprint, along with many other rare tracts, all however in the original tongue, which is in many cases Latin. Nevertheless the venture is of the first importance to students at all levels; the Mathew Hopkins material, for instance, is in English, as are Glanvil, Mather, and others on the list, or likely to be so.

The first of the classical demonologists, chronologically at least, is Nicholas Jacquier, a Dominican inquisitor. He is the author of two important works, *Tractatus de Calcatione Demonum*, written in 1452, an attack on various heresies, and *Flagellum Haereticorum Fascinarium*, written in 1458, but known only from a publication in 1581. This book was one of many written to undermine the *Canon Episcopi*; it is extensively quoted by Lea (*Materials*, 1:275-86).

Next comes the *Malleus Maleficarum*, 1486 (the date is not absolutely certain, by the way), which we have already covered. After that, I should cite the work of Sylvester Prierias, another Dominican; as the most considerable in the main tradition: *De Strigamagarum Daemonumque Mirandis*, 1521. Again Lea has the fullest commentary; for some reason Robbins has no separate entry on this important writer. He is mentioned however in Robbins's entry for "Ointment, flying" (p. 364). Lea says that "he is fully imbued with the doctrines of the *Malleus Maleficarum*, which he quotes" (1:358). Prierias was an eminent man, the papal champion against Luther, yet his writings are notable for their extreme credulity: for instance, on the subject of intercourse between human beings and spirits, he cites Venus and Anchises. He may be found listed by Summers under his family name, Mazzolini.

A student of Prierias's, Bartolommeo Spina, produced an important book, *Quaestio de Strigibus*, in 1523. Summers also cites with approval his *Tractatus de Strigibus et Lamiis*, of 1533. Spina was yet another learned Dominican, who had a large hand in the persecutions of Northern Italy; he always insisted on the reality of the witches' experiences, thus denying the *Canon Episcopi*. Large entry in Lea, smaller citation in Robbins.

We come next to Paulus Grillandus and his book *Tractatus de Hereticis et Sortilegiis*, 1536,[8] which Robbins calls "after the *Malleus Maleficarum*, probably the most influential work on witchcraft published before the middle of the sixteenth century."[9] With Grillandus we enter the courtroom proper; he was himself a papal judge who presided over witch-trials at Rome. Robbins heaps scorn upon him; says that by his efforts "the fabric of witchcraft was buttressed by the crassest fables of the preceding century. And yet Grillandus was a Doctor of Laws."[10] Other modern authorities are more respectful: Summers, of course, who often quotes "the erudite Paul Grilland" in his *History*, and Kittredge, who using the Italian form (thus in his index), also goes often to "the evidence of the distinguished Florentine jurist Paolo Grillando." "The cool prose of his catalogue of horrors," Kittredge says, "makes the thing as vivid as it is gruesome."[11] At the start of a long entry on Grillandus (1:395-412), Lea notes that in his dedication of his *Tractatus* (to Felix, Archbishop Chieti), he gives as his reason for writing, his concern over the growth of the "pernicious sect," and the fact that so many of the clergy are embroiled in it. Many of the facts which Grillandus gives are warranted as first-hand experience; he actually handled witches' ointments, for example. Lea thinks that he did not depend so much upon earlier authors as upon his own observations, which makes him an especially valuable source of data, although not one, as Robbins reminds us, to be read without caution.

Pedro Cirvelo's *Opus de Magica Superstitione*, 1521, is particularly noteworthy in that its translation in 1539 makes it the first witchcraft book in Spanish, and "The classical one in Spain," according to Lea (1:413). Cirvelo was an inquisitor of thirty years' experience, in Saragossa, and canon of Salamanca.

Our next author, and a most important one, is another jurist, the renowned Jean Bodin, whose works are often cited by modern scholars in support of their various positions. His two most important books are *De la Démonomanie de Sorciers*, published in French in 1580, and *Le Fléau des Demons et Sorciers*, 1616. Summers calls him "one of the acutest and most strictly impartial men of his age,"[12] although his subsequent research somewhat tempers his enthusiasm.[13] For Pennethorne Hughes Bodin is "the great authority of the seventeenth century."[14] Margaret Murray cites him frequently, although the peculiarities of her index in *The Witch-Cult* preclude his appearance there. (He is listed in her bibliography.) Robbins calls his *Démonomanie* "a horrible landmark," and asserts that for the most part he "writes as an unmitigated bigot,"[15] at least upon witchcraft.

The fact is that Bodin was not "a defender of authority and belief," as Hughes says,[16] but both a liberal, almost a radical, in politics, for which he lost royal favor; and a conciliator in religion, for which he saw his books placed on the Index. He presents remarkably strong confirmation of one of Kittredge's favorite points, that some of the finest and best minds of previous ages, notable for a precocious enlightment in certain areas, may yet reveal what are to us most horrible aspects of cruelty, bigotry, and superstition. One can only wonder what succeeding generations will make of us. Robbins may be questioned for calling Bodin's beliefs bigoted, but he is certainly warranted in focusing his disapproval on his judicial practice, which was both cruel and unfeeling. Bodin's great prestige as professor of Law (University of Toulouse), courtier, public prosecutor, and learned writer aided the spread of his opinions. As Lea reminds us, Pierre Bayle thought Bodin the ablest writer in France, while Montaigne called him the highest literary genius of his time (2:554).

A great German authority is Peter Binsfeld, Suffragan Bishop of Trier, a theologian and teacher. His text is called *Tractatus de Confessionibus Maleficorum et Sagarum*, 1589; it was extended in the later editions with another of his works, *Commentarius in Titulum Codicis Lib. IX de Maleficis et Mathematicis, etc.*, 1591. Of these writings, Lea remarks, "the coolness with which the necessary premises are assumed, and the ingenuity with which texts in favor are construed to the strictest letter and those adverse are explained away, are only equalled by the logical strictness of the deductions" (2:579-80).

Our next man is Nicholas Remy, the second of the great quartet of master demonologists of France (Bodin, Remy, Boguet, de Lancre). His magnum opus is *Demonolatreiae*, 1595. On the title page, Remy, a judge, boasts of having condemned nine hundred witches. He was one of a family of lawyers, and later attorney general of Lorraine, a cultivated man, a scholar and a poet. In his writings on witchcraft, however, it is the prosecutor in him which is closest to the surface. Lea thinks his book "perhaps the most vivid picture of the beliefs and cruelty of the period, as his statements are all authenticated with the names and dates of the victims whose confessions he received during the fifteen years in which he had officiated as judge" (2:604). Thus the advantages attached to books by practicing jurists, rather than speculative clergymen. *Demonolatreiae* even superceded the *Malleus* to an extent, according to Lea. It is a fascinating document; Summers translated it into English in 1930. In a sense it is also Remy's memoirs, as Charles Williams remarks,[17] in which the old judge muses about his career, lamenting, among other things, that he had shown too much tenderness to children (scourging three times naked around the stake where one's mother has been burned is not punishment enough; death is the only real remedy).

If Remy's book became for a time the most prestigious in the field, it was quickly superceded by the massive work of the Jesuit Martin Del Rio, *Disquisitionum Magicarum*, 1599, which Robbins calls "in many ways the most complete of all the works on witchcraft."[18] Del Rio was a Spanish aristocrat, born in the Low Countries (Antwerp), and "a prodigy of learning," according to his contemporaries (Lea, 2:640). Such disproportionate praise has now given way to almost complete neglect; even Summers, who quotes him five times in his *History*, does not hail him with the same enthusiasm which he usually shows for the old writers. The best summary of his work is in Lea, volume 2, pages 640-46; and even this is less than a third of the space given Remy.

Henri Boguet is the third of the great French demonologists. He was also a judge, president of the tribunal of Saint-Claude, Burgundy. "It has been calculated that he ordered at least six hundred executions," Summers tells us, "many of these being upon charges of lycanthropy" *(Geography*, p. 405). His great work, abbreviated as *Discours des Sorciers*, 1602, was of particular value to his contemporaries because of its appendix, "The manner of Procedure of a Judge in a Case of Witchcraft." Like Remy, Boguet approved the extreme penalty for juvenile sorcerers, and he is on record as having had an eight-year-old girl "systematically tortured."[19]

Less original than many of his predecessors, but even more credulous, was Francesco-Maria Guazzo (or Guaccio, as in Lea, or Guazzi), whose book, *Compendium Maleficarum*, 1608, nevertheless became influential, largely because it was indeed a compendium of earlier writings. Robbins has a good if brief account of Guazzo, a Milanese friar and assessor in witchcraft trials. All the wildest tales of the preceding texts found a home in Guazzo, who tells of the offspring of a "lewd fellow" and a cow, who felt in himself "certain bovine propensities, as that of eating grass and chewing the cud" (Robbins, pp. 236-37). He also reports the monstrous results of the union between a man and a monkey. As Lea remarks, "The credulity of the period was insatiable" (2:918).

Pierre de Lancre completes our list of French master-demonologists. He is a hero to Summers, who says, "It must be remembered that de Lancre was a scholar, a patron and follower of the fine arts, a writer of no inconsiderable power and precision, a clear-headed shrewd observer of men and manners."[20] Indeed the man is fully worthy of his high place in Summers's calendar; as a trial judge he boasted of his six hundred victims. At one point he found that the entire population of Labourd, some thirty thousand, has succumbed to witchcraft, clergy and all.

The rich detail of his *Tableau*[21] has made it a principal source for many scholars; Summers says of it and de Lancre's other books, "These writings are of the greatest value, and I have largely relied upon them in my account of the Sabbat and other evil practices of the witches in the sixteenth and seventeenth centuries."[22] Margaret Murray quotes de Lancre more, I should guess (without counting her citations), than any other source. Lea has an extensive section on the *Tableau* (3:1292-1304). Under "Ancre, Pierre de 1'," we find a dozen citations of him by Kittredge,[23] although mostly in notes of reference.

With Joseph Glanvil, we are really come upon the rearguard; he is not perhaps properly referred to at this point, but as a wholehearted adherent to the orthodox party, and an Englishman, of a race not yet represented on our list, he is I think worthy of mention here. His book is called *Saducismus Triumphatus*, 1681. It was much reprinted, and edited by the celebrated Henry More, a firm believer in Glanvil's revelations;[24] consequently, and by virtue of the fact that it is in English, it is one of the more easily acquired of the old witchcraft texts. The third edition of 1700, with More's remarks and additions, plus the accounts of the Swedish trials at Mora, is a particularly desirable one.

Although Robbins nominates him as "the father of modern psychical research,"[25] it is possible to see Glanvil as just one of the more able, late rationalizers of Satan's invisible world. His objectivity is not really of much use to him, despite his good intentions. His collections of facts are interesting to modern readers, however, as are all the details appended to the later editions.

The man generally considered the last of the orthodox school is Ludovico Maria Sinistrari, a Franciscan. He gets good marks from Robbins (who is generally severe upon the demonologists), as one "known in his own day as a scholar and a gentleman, a good linguist and an urbane conversationalist." This quote is from a very short notice in Robbins's *Encyclopedia* (p. 470); Lea has a slightly longer citation (2:919-22). The book is *De Daemonialitate,* but it was not published as such in his lifetime. Most of the material in it was available to his contemporaries as part of his *De Delictis et Poenis* (1700), a major work on crime and punishment. As "Sinistrari d' Ameno" (he was born in Ameno), he is cited at some length by Summers: "a scholar of immense erudition," etc.[26]

These are the principal fabricators of the orthodox position on witchcraft, which is to say, the conventional idea of witchcraft; they should be known to every student in the field. The following is another short list of authors of secondary importance who are also of interest:

Johannes Nider, *Formicarius,* written ca. 1435, printed 1475, an early and valuable work. Lacks classic features, as pact, sabbat, transvection. Robbins calls Nider "almost a skeptic."[27]

Alphonso de Spina, *Fortalicium Fidei,* 1464, 1467? (written 1458-60). No separate entry in Robbins; fairly large citation in Lea (1:285-92). Early, detailed disquisition on demons, their nature and habits.

Heinrich Molitor, *De Lamiis et Phitonicis Mulieribus,* 1489. Molitor a disciple of Kramer and Sprenger. Zealous and intemperate advocate of witch persecution.

Ludwig Lavater, *De Spectris* (shortened title), 1569. Lavater a Swiss, his first edition in German. Protestant minister. A specialist on demons, not witches, but "no disbeliever in the power of sorcery" (Lea, 2:553). No entry in Robbins.

Sabastien Michaelis, *Pneumalogie* (shortened), 1587. Dominican, minor French demonologist. Interesting details: Sabbats only take place on Thursdays. Not in Robbins as separate entry.

Benedict Carpzov, *Practica Rerum Criminalium,* 1635. A singularly bloodthirsty judge, one of most notable figures in history of witchcraft, but not for his book, which treats of criminal jurisprudence in general. Very long entry in Lea (2:813-50), major citation in Robbins, who calls him a "a ruthless bigot" (*Encyclopedia*, p. 78). Carpzov was a German Protestant, reputed to have signed death warrants of 20,000 people.

Richard Bovet, *Pandaemonium*, 1684. An English country squire, very minor demonologist of a charming credulity. Admired the great Glanvil. Summers had *Pandaemonium*, which is extremely rare in first edition (9 known copies) reprinted in 1951. Pleasant reading (especially after Carpzov).

The following men are noteworthy as the principal founders and supporters of the skeptical position, for taking which they put themselves in danger of their lives. They were not always effective, because they did not, for the most part, challenge the witchcraft belief in any of its basic tenets, such as the existence of evil spirits. Even so, the records of the controversies raised by their courageous opposition to the prevailing hysteria, and the data gathered by them, are valuable material for the student today.

We ought to distinguish between those who opposed the first formulations of the heresy, and those who fought the delusion at its height. Among the first, Robbins tells us, there were only three writers of major stature who opposed the *Malleus:* "Symphorien Champier (about 1500), Samuel de Cassini (about 1505), and Gianfrancesco Ponzinibio (about 1520)."[28] Of these, I should think Ponzinibio the most important, because his book, *Tractatus de Lamiis* (shortened), ca. 1520, excited the most interest; in fact it evoked a major controversy.

Ponzinibio believed in sorcery, but he repudiated the legal methods being developed to deal with it; furthermore he dismissed many of the key aspects of witchcraft as fantasy. For this he was bitterly attacked by the orthodox, whose writings, unfortunately, are our major source of information about this little-known man. Bartolommeo Spina, who wrote to refute him, wanted to prosecute him as an accessory. In fact he was a fit adversary for the inquisitors; Lea speaks of his "minute and prolonged argumentation, every step of which is abundantly fortified by citation of authorities and texts of civil and canon law" (1:379). His base was the *Canon Episcopi*, that stumbling block over which the witchfinders were ever seeking to rise. But his worst offense was his suggestion that legal science was superior to theological science, and should therefore hold preeminence of place at the trials. It was for this most of all that Spina attacked him. All we know for sure of Ponzinibio is that he was Italian, and a lawyer; his book calls him a Florentine, but in it he refers to himself as coming from Piacenza.[29]

Champier was a physician, who took the point of view that many of the reports of witchcraft could be explained medically. His *Dialogus* (shortened), ca. 1500, is hard to come by. He has a small citation in Lea (1:354); no separate entry in Robbins. Samuel de Cassini, a Franciscan, attacked witchcraft beliefs on logical grounds: "The gist of his argument," Lea says, "is that the flight of witches would be a miracle" (1:366). He also put his trust in the *Canon Episcopi*, going so far as to accuse the inquisitors themselves of heavy sin, even heresy. His book, *Question de le Strie*, ca. 1505, did not however have much effect upon orthodoxy, as far as I can gather.

It is the later writers who really took their lives in their hands. Of these, perhaps the most celebrated is Johan Weyer (Wier, Wierus, etc.). He was a Dutch physician, and a most humane man, who opposed the trials more "by pity than by reason," as Robbins puts it.[30] For this reason, he was easily refuted by his infuriated opponents, notably Bodin, who would have burned him except for the protection of the Duke of Cleves. His theology was shaky; his doctrines "have a half-hearted appearance,"[31] as Kittredge observes, because he did himself believe in devils and spirits. Nevertheless his humanity was strong, and his common sense stronger still. His books *De Praestigiis Daemonum* (shortened), 1563, and *De Lamiis*, 1577, consistently pour doubt on the witchfinders' data as illusions, fantasies, and deceits of the Devil, who is the real benefiter by the persecutions. We know that Weyer was able to bring his influence to bear upon the cruelties of the trials; often he speaks of people whose lives he has saved. As Kittredge says, he "deserves all the honor he has ever received."[32]

Next is our own Reginald Scot, whose *Discovery of Witchcraft*, 1584, is the first book on the subject in English. We have already had occasion to notice Scot because of his learning (he opposed the tendency to translate all sorts of biblical malefactors as "witches"); he is also notable for wit, fine spirited common sense, a flair for raillery, and a most lively style. Shakespeare seems to have been among the many who consulted him. Nevertheless we must remember that he was to a great extent restricted by the fact that he shared his contemporaries' belief in the spiritual world; and therefore we should not be surprised that his book was not as convincing to King James as it is to us.[33] An excellent modern text of the *Discovery* was recently published (Southern Illinois University Press, 1964).

"Father Cornelius Loos, the first man in Germany who raised his voice against the witch hunts," according to Robbins, "was a celebrated theologian; he was tortured and banished."[34] And came within an ace of being burned, would have been, probably, had not natural death intervened. Like Weyer, who may have influenced him, Loos was Dutch. It was the fierce cruelty of the trials that stirred him to write; when he did so (*De Vera et Falsa Magia* [True and False Magic], 1592), he was arrested and jailed. His recantation was written for him by Binsfeld, the man he had attacked; and the Jesuit Del Rio printed it in his *Disquisition*. *Vera et Falsa Magia* was so well suppressed that it never did come out in his lifetime; the manuscript was discovered by George Lincoln Burr in the City Library at Trier in 1886. Lea calls Loos "a worthy colleague of Reginald Scot" (2:604).

Another such man is the saintly Friedrich Spee, a Jesuit to balance Del Rio (whom he confutes in print). Spee was confessor to the accused during some of the worst witch trials in Germany (Wurzburg, 1620s); Leibnitz reports that his hair turned white from grief at having accompanied so many witches to the stake—and thinking none of them guilty.[35] His *Cautio Criminalis* (1631) is "a stringent indictment of the German princes and judges who encouraged the atrocities."[36] It is also a powerful attack on the standard authorities, particularly Del Rio of his own order, and an appeal to logic: all these confessions are based on torture, Spee says, and are therefore worthless.

Spee died at forty-four of the plague, caught from parishioners he was attending; and thus perhaps escaped a different end. He was incredibly outspoken. Burr produces evidence that he may have been imprisoned at one time.[37] It seems almost unbelievable that he could have escaped all punishment[38] after having written what Kittredge proclaims "the most powerful and convincing protest against witch trials ever written."[39]

Our last skeptic is Balthasar Bekker: "here at last we have a rational method," Kittredge says.[40] Bekker was still another Dutchman, all honor to them. One reason he could "lay the axe to the root" (Kittredge), was that he was writing a good hundred years and more after Scot and Weyer. His *De Betoverde Weereld* [Enchanted World] appeared in 1691 and 1693 (books 1 and 2 had appeared in 1690, according to Lea [3:1392]). Something of a baroque Sir James Frazer, Bekker begins his study with a broad survey of beliefs among ancient and modern peoples. He continues through a dispassionate survey of the Bible, coming to the conclusion that since Eden, the Devil has played no part at all in the daily lives of men. And so on, through all the articles of the witchcraft faith.

Holland was a better place than many in Europe as regards witch persecutions; nevertheless, even there, at a time when hysteria had almost run its course, Bekker found himself in deep trouble. He was declared "intolerable as teacher in the Reformed Church" and expelled from his ministerial office, in 1692. A week or so later he was additionally denied communion, which he never received again.[41]

There were thousands upon thousands of witch trials, of which a small number have become famous. At this point I wish to cite a few with which the student should be familiar. All but one are well represented in the encyclopedists who have played such an important part in this chapter, and on whom most students must depend in the study of early texts and events. In succeeding chapters I shall introduce other trials, appropriate to the subject matter under discussion; here it will be fitting to examine, very briefly, some trials notable for their classic features.

The first is, appropriately enough, a German trial, that of Dietrich Flade, in Trier, 1588-89. A series of natural calamities, aggravated by the harassments of robbers and guerrilla warfare, had set the area seething; a scapegoat was necessary. Flade, a most eminent citizen, Rector of the University and the head of the secular courts of Trier, is a classic example of the man who, in trying to restrain popular fury against a minority, becomes associated with that minority, and finally suffers with them. Burr, who uncovered the records of the case, called him witchburning's "most eminent victim in the land of its greatest thoroughness."[42]

The case against Flade is reproduced in an excellent entry in Robbins's *Encyclopedia* (pp. 201-5). The judge was no hero, nor even a particularly thoughtful man; he accepted witchcraft fully in theory. But the cruelties of the prosecutors, particularly the bloodthirsty Bishop Peter Binsfeld and Governor Johann Zandt, appalled him, and he resisted them. "He became an obstacle," Robbins notes, and "had to be removed." How Zandt built up a case against him, full of the wildest accusations, including presence at the Sabbat, eating fritters made of children's hearts, and causing plagues of hailstones and snails, is fully reproduced in the *Encyclopedia*. On September 18, 1589, Flade was burned, after having been first "mercifully and Christianly strangled."

My next example is also from Germany, and an even more famous case. It is that of the werewolf Peter Stubbe (Stump, Stumpf, etc.), captured, tried, and executed near Cologne in 1589. Our best source for these events is a pamphlet "of the last rarity," published in London the year after Stubbe's execution. It is called *A True Discourse. Declaring the damnable life and death of one Stubbe Peeter, a most wicked Sorcerer, who in the likeness of a Woolfe, committed many murders, continuing this deuelish practise 25 yeeres, killing and deuouring Men, Woomen, and Children. Who for the same fact was taken and executed the 31. of October last past in the town of Bedbur neer the Cittie of Collin in Germany.* Montague Summers, author of the comment above, reproduced this tract in full, with the old illustrations, as an appendix to his book *The Werewolf* (London, 1933, p. 253-59).

For once Summers's indignation is compelling. It seems likely that Stubbe did commit all or at least many of the outrages with which he was charged—although popular report credited him with an immense slaughter of women and children as well as lambs and kids, plus an assortment of sexual irregularities, it is significant that the tract ends by speaking of the "sixteene persons that was perfectly known to be murdered by him." Setting aside the numerous details of his trafficking with the Devil, it seems pretty clear that he was an authentic lycanthrope, of a kind still occasionally to be met with in the newspapers, and was well put out of the way, although one recoils at the severity of the punishment:

> Stubbe Peeter as principal mallefactor, was judged first to haue his body laid on a wheele, and with red hotte burning pincers in ten seueral places to haue the flesh puld off from the bones, after that, his legges and Armes to be broken with a woodden Axe or Hatchet, afterward to haue his head strook from his body, then to haue his carkasse burnde to Ashes. (P. 259)

Our next trial is English, and thus much less sensational than the last two, although wild enough. It is the case of the Warboys Witches, in Huntingdon, 1593, one of the key English trials, the most celebrated in that country before 1600 according to Robbins, who introduces it as "a notorious plot against three innocent people" (*Encyclopedia*, p. 527). One of the most widely reported and commented-upon trials, it presents a good text for the student. There are solid accounts in Wallace Notestein, Kittredge, Hughes, and Christina Hole (*Witchcraft in England* [London, 1945], pp. 39-40). The case in many ways sets the pattern for the English-speaking world: hysterical child accusers, heard by their foolish elders as oracles; a poor credulous, slightly daft old woman persecuted by the offspring of the well-to-do; spectral evidence, fits in court—all the important elements of the Salem trials are present. The result was, three people hanged. Their goods were seized by the lord of the manor (whose wife was said to have died bewitched) and used to subsidize an annual sermon against witchcraft, which was given until 1812, though in its latter days, as a warning against belief.[43]

Another important trial, or series of trials, are those of Labourd, in the Basque country of France, 1609. This is de Lancre's show, presented by him with such detail in his *Tableau*. Robbins has a good account of the proceedings under the heading "Basque Witches," page 40. We have already spoken of de Lancre's feats in some detail; it remains to observe that his wholesale condemnations excited wholesale reprisal; finally the bishop himself joined the opposition, and rescued five priests from jail (three had already been burned). De Lancre's authority was special, direct from the king, and he was accountable to no one else—another telling example of the consequences of departing from established procedures in capital cases, or perhaps any other.

We ought to include here one of the great French convent cases, of which that of Urbain Grandier at Loudun (1634) is the most celebrated example. Reserving that one for the chapter on psychological aspects, we might mention the case of 1611 at Aix-en-Provence. Here we meet with the classic symptoms: a whole convent full of bewitched nuns (sexually starved and hysterical), a handsome father-confessor accused of trafficking with the Devil, intrigue in high places, political and clerical maneuvering, and victims slaughtered for public edification. Sabastien Michaelis was the inquisitor involved; his published findings provide "one of the most detailed accounts of prolonged daily exorcisms . . . ever written."[44]

Taking advantage of the lax moral climate of the times, Father Louis Gaufridi, parish priest of Accoules in Marseilles, contracted a liaison with a beautiful fourteen-year-old, Madeleine Demandolx, the spoiled child of a wealthy and aristocratic family. Madeleine, who was also deeply religious, later entered a convent where she fell victim to all sorts of hallucinations and fears, no doubt as the combined result of guilt and longing. Eventually she infected other nuns with her symptoms and Gaufridi was summoned before the inquisitors, who were reluctantly forced to let him go, in the face of a total lack of evidence against him. Madeleine's behavior grew still worse, however, verging upon actual madness—Robbins suggests a manic-depressive state (p. 23), and Father Gaufridi was haled into the civil courts, much the worse for his year-and-a-half's interrogation by the inquisition. Under torture he confessed everything, the pact with Evil, all; but later recanted, and was horribly tortured again. Robbins has the details. Eventually he was strangled (as a favor) and burned. Madeleine was "cured," but in later life was herself arrested and imprisoned as a witch.

Every bit as bad—in fact, worse—was the prolonged witch-hunt in Bamberg, Germany, between 1609 and 1631, fanned to its height by the greedy Prince-Bishop Johann George II (1623-33), who gained vast wealth from burning some six hundred of the citizens of his bishopric, including many of the wealthiest and most highly-placed. These trials are key ones in the skeptical case, for obvious reasons: rarely was official rapacity so nakedly displayed. All the burgomasters were burned, Robbins says (p. 36). Most noteworthy among them was Johannes Junius, who managed to smuggle out of prison a letter to his daughter, telling of his treatment at the hands of the authorities. Incredibly, it has survived, and may be read today in Robbins's *Encyclopedia* (pp. 292-93). It is a horrifying and moving document, as bad as anything out of the Nazi extermination camps.

For a long time there was no stopping the bishop; letters from the Kaiser did no good, and when a local official like Vice-Chancellor George Haan tried to slow the process, he was himself seized and burned, with all his family. Pressure from all over the Empire was brought on Bamberg, but the persecutions did not stop until the bishop's death.

It is refreshing to turn from these scenes of horror to another case which, bad as it is, at least does not present the accusers in a worse light than the accused. As with Peter Stubbe, there can be little doubt that the Countess Elizabeth Bathory did, like Gilles de Rais (whom we shall consider in the next chapter), preside over the kidnapping and murder of children, over one hundred in her case, aided by all the trappings of sorcery and demonolatry.

She does not appear in the standard works, because her case lies somewhat aside from the main line of witchcraft studies. It was resuscitated by William Seabrook, always a curious researcher in occult fields, from a book in the original Hungarian, stored up in the New York Public Library. Seabrook had the countess' story translated, and published a lengthy account of it in his book *Witchcraft* (New York, 1940, pp. 115-27). He calls her "World Champion Lady Vampire of all times," and adds, "she also practiced magic and was a witch."

Her wealth and high position allowed her to carry on her evil practices (Seabrook says she was a coven leader) for years without much interference, until gradually her outrages grew insupportable, and on New Year's Eve, 1610, her castle in Bitcse, Carpathia, was raided by a combined force of police and soldiers, led by her own cousin, Count Gyorgy Thurzo, the governor of the province. What they found was right out of a horror movie script: young girls in various stages of bleeding, some dead, some pierced with needles, some being tortured. Others were being fattened in the dungeon, and many bodies were exhumed. For ten years the Countess had been bathing in human blood to keep her beauty fresh; Seabrook estimated that she killed between "80 and 300." (Ornella Volta gives the number 600, although on dubious authority.)[45]

The case was disposed of in a straightforward manner: first, the trial was criminal, not ecclesiastical, so that the facts were not obscured by metaphysics or confessions of sabbats and so forth, although a paper was found which invoked demonic aid. Countess Bathory's accomplices were given summary justice. Those who had aided her merely as procurers (mostly her own menials) were decapitated and burned to ashes. Her chief helpers, two old women specifically called witches, were dismembered—their fingers were torn off—and then burned alive. The Countess herself was not touched, whether out of superstitious fear or reverence for her position. She was instead walled up alive in her own castle, where she died four years later, in 1614.

A more central case, and one of the best documented that we have, is that of Eichstätt, Germany, in 1637. "For any reader who wants to understand witchcraft," Robbins writes, "this record gives a very clear introduction" *(Encyclopedia,* p. 149). The entire account as written down by the court scribe is in existence, although with the names of the principals deleted. Robbins's summary is an excellent cameo of the skeptical view:

> In this trial, the procedure follows every approved cliché of witchdom: the accused first denies, then is tortured; she invents what she thinks the judges want; then, released from the torture, she recants her confession, and straightway is tortured again. Soon she becomes half demented and ends up by believing herself a witch.[46]

In fact the substitution of letters for names—the accused is called "N.N."—does bring the whole affair close to reading like an academic exercise, one of Carpzov's or Sprenger's manuals of procedure.

An even more important case to the skeptics is that of Lindheim, Germany again, in 1663-64, when Johann Schüler and his wife, along with many more totally innocent persons, were seized, tortured, and abused with the utmost brutality. Robbins is moved to call the case "the most atrocious in this *Encyclopedia*" (p. 449).

It seems to have been a simple matter of the local noblemen and churchmen yielding to the suggestions of a certain magistrate, one Geiss, that they could all fill their pockets by instituting a witch-hunt, with him in charge. This they did forthwith, and Geiss and his picked assistants, "four of the lowest and most vicious scum of the town" (Robbins, p. 450), proceeded to torture and burn with abandon. Schüler's wife was arrested on the usual trumped-up charges and burned before her husband could get help (he himself had been severely tortured, but had escaped). The only thing that could put a stop to the outrages of the gang was a popular rising, which forced them to leave town. The details of their work are in print for the curious, but we have had about enough.

One more trial, then, and we shall have done: This one is Swedish, and the most celebrated one ever held in Scandinavia; the place is Mora, the year 1669. A full account from the original documents may be found appended to Glanvil's *Saducismus Triumphatus*, 1700 edition. The affair is remarkable for its suddenness and violence: eighty-five people were burned in all, adults for having "drawn some hundreds of children" into witchcraft, carrying them off to the Sabbat, and all the rest. The whole population flew into hysteria; and despite the mild injunction of the king, Charles XI, to pray for the afflicted, the usual bloodbath followed. Some of the older children were burned; younger ones were punished by having to run the gauntlet; and little ones were let off with weekly floggings over a year's time.

The trials cited in this chapter are particularly well-suited to illustrate the orthodox and skeptical positions. They inspire horror and indignation in those who report them, whether on account of the unspeakable crimes of the accused—which in the cases of Countess Elizabeth Bathory and Peter Stubbe seem to be well-documented—or because of the unspeakable crimes of the accusers, which certainly appear to be beyond doubt in the cases of

Dietrich Flade and Johannes Junius. Of course trials may be seen in other ways; certain among them are of great importance to the anthropologists, the psychologists, and the pharmacologists; we shall need to look at many more of these cases in the chapters to come. But for the moment let there be no more. One feels (if the reader will forgive the comparison) like Byron's recording angels:

> They threw their pens down in divine disgust—
> The page was so besmear'd with blood and dust.

6. The Anthropological Position

 Montague Summers should be familiar, by now, as the latter-day champion of orthodoxy. Indeed very few, even in the days when the witch-hunts were at their height, surpassed him in fervor against the witches and the designs of their master Satan. How it would have galled him to find the introduction to the second edition of his *History of Witchcraft* (New York, 1956) written by an avowed disciple of the anthropological school! O Thief in the house of the just!

Felix Morrow, the gentleman in question, writing just a few years after Summers's death (1948), begins his foreword in this manner:

> In the pages of this book the reader will quite often come across the name of Margaret A. Murray and it will become clear to him that she is Summers's great antagonist. True, he waxes almost warm toward her when he adduces her common stand with him that witchcraft was widespread and really believed in by friend and foe alike, as against the "liberal" historians [called "Skeptics" in this book—C.A.H.] who think of it as at most a temporary madness. Beyond that, however, Miss Murray's views are obviously anathema. However, Summers never makes precisely clear what these views are.
>
> I share Miss Murray's views, in the main, and I think it important for the reader to understand what they are. She has made them very clear in two splendid books, *The Witch Cult of [sic] Western Europe,* and *The God of the Witches,* and in very compact form in the article on Witchcraft in the

recent editions of the *Encyclopaedia Britannica*. I should like
to believe that the choice of Miss Murray to write the
Encyclopaedia article means that her views have now
prevailed, but unfortunately it is not so.

Morrow then quotes Margaret Murray briefly and sums up this
portion of his remarks:

> "When examining the records of the medieval witches, we
> are dealing with the remains of a pagan religion which
> survived, in England at least, until the eighteenth century,
> twelve hundred years after the introduction of Christianity.
> The practices of the ancient faith can be found in France at
> the present day; and in Italy *la vecchia religione* (the old
> religion) still numbers many followers in spite of the efforts
> of the Christian churches."
>
> The pagan religion of the witches of Europe, when
> described without prejudice, is quite familiar to any reader
> of *The Golden Bough* or other anthropological material.
> Central to it is a god incarnate in a human being or an
> animal, appearing to his worshippers dressed in black or
> disguised in various animal forms, the appearances being at
> assemblies or *sabbaths*. The sexual orgies reveled in by
> Summers appear quite differently when Miss Murray
> reminds us how similiar they are to the sacred marriage of
> the Greeks or the Saturnian revels of the Romans. . . . Miss
> Murray's endlessly fascinating material is available easily
> enough to interested readers. The point here is that she does
> establish to our satisfaction that what has come down to us
> under the name of witchcraft was a religion of the people
> which was overcome by Christianity, and, in defeat, had its
> terminology and the description of its rites defined for it and
> posterity by the victors. (Pp. vii-viii)

Aside from its convenience as a summation, this passage is
valuable as an example of what we may call "maleficography," or
the study of witchcraft-study. In this field, the eruption of the
anthropologists in 1921 (the date of the *Witch-Cult*) was the most
important event in several centuries. Since the decline of orthodoxy

in the eighteenth century, and the almost complete triumph of skepticism in the nineteenth, witchcraft studies had lapsed into somnolence, broken only by the gentle and regular breathing forth of academic exercises. When Murray published, and was followed immediately (1922) by *The Golden Bough,* the world perceived a whole new way of looking at data accumulated over the centuries, and the subject came alive again.[1]

We may distinguish between three central responses to these revelations: first, the emergence of a whole school of believers, and a strong impetus to scholarship; second, the reinvigoration of the skeptics, grown tame in their ascendance; and third, a new era of prosperity among occultists, on whom Murray and Frazer appeared to put the seal of respectability. From this period we may date the beginnings of the stream of coven-confessions and witch-autobiographies which has today reached flood proportion.

Frazer's classical matrix was of particular service to witchcraft students, who were able to call upon all the Greek and Roman documents, some of which we have looked at, to show that well-defined fertility cults, closely resembling witchcraft, did indeed exist in the ancient world. Others went back further still into the realm of early man, whose cave drawings represent him as the occasional occupant of ritual-purpose animal-skins and horned headdresses. The point of departure for almost all of these studies was Margaret Murray's original book, *The Witch-Cult in Western Europe,* whose main tendency we have just had summed up for us. At this point we should become familiar with her more particular observations.

She divides her study into six main parts (following her section 1, the "continuity of the religion"). These are devoted to the god of the witches, the admission ceremonies to his worship, the witch assemblies, the rites, the organization of the religion, and familiars and transformation. She adds appendices on fairies, certain trials, witches' names, and flying ointments, some of which material, considerably enlarged, becomes the basis of her next book, *The God of the Witches* (1931).

As to him worshiped by the witches, Murray finds that he was not Satan, nor Beelzebub; these were the names the Christians gave him. To members of the cult he was truly their god and lord, as

Murray gathers from data drawn from our friends Boguet, de Lancre, and Glanvil, among others. The aspects of his worship which the inquisitors found so repellent she sees as natural and reasonable in the survival of a fertility cult: copulation with the god, for example, or his priest, which is mentioned in so many old accounts, as well as sexual promiscuity throughout the cult. According to much testimony, intercourse with "the Devil" was painful; his member was cold and hard, his sperm icy; Margaret Murray believes that these details indicate the use of an artificial phallus. The fact that the god also would frequently appear as an animal—buck, goat, or bull—explains the Christian charges of bestiality.

The essence of the admission ceremonies, Murray says, are these: "first, that the candidates must join of their own free will and without compulsion; the second, that they devote themselves, body and soul, to the Master and his service" (p. 71). Parents, especially mothers, brought their children, especially daughters, into the cult by old customs (perhaps dating back to the matriarchal age?). This explains the Christians' tendency to pursue the issue through families, which at first seems wanton cruelty, but was actually based upon a good understanding of the way the cult worked. During the great persecutions, having one of your relatives burned was among the worst of omens. Witches' marks, so often searched for by inquisitors, may also be seen as a part of ancient ritual.

Murray distinguishes between two kinds of witches' assemblies: the Sabbath, "The General Meeting of all the members of the religion" and the "Esbat," which she cites on the slender authority of one writer, Estabene de Cambrue (whom she found quoted in de Lancre); this was for the inner circle. The Esbat was "primarily for business, whereas the Sabbath was purely religious" (p. 112). Both of these were nocturnal, and those attending relied mostly upon ordinary means of transportation, although old tradition credits witches with the power to fly to them from afar, either on sticks or animals of various kinds, after having anointed themselves with ointment. A.J. Clark, in an appendix to *The Witch-Cult*, deals in more detail with these ointments and suggests that they may give the sensation of flight. Surely straddling animals or phallic broomsticks is an understandable feature of a fertility cult.

The rites "probably varied in different localities," but Murray is able to lay out a typical sabbat (which she believes to have no connection etymologically with the Jewish word; "it is possibly a derivative of *s'esbattre*, 'to folic,'" p. 97). [2] The order of proceedings is as follows: worshipers pay homage to their lord ("The Devil"); with vows, obeisance, sacred kisses and ritual movement (dancing "widdershins," counterclockwise); members report and consult about their (magical) activities; then neophytes are admitted, and marriages are performed. The business portion of the meeting being concluded, the religious ceremony follows, appropriate to the season of the year; this includes the "obscene" fertility rites. "The whole ceremony ended with feasting and dancing, and the assembly broke up at dawn" (p. 124). The Esbat "had less ceremonial, and the religious service was not performed" (p. 124).

Among other details of note in Margaret Murray's discussion of these practices is her statement that child sacrifice was certainly practiced, as a typical fertility rite; that the child was "usually a young infant" not belonging to the Christian community (p. 156). Thus the insistence on infant baptism, which to the Christians would protect their children from diabolic menace, but which to the pagans would make worthless an otherwise appropriate offering to the god of generation.

Also very significant to Murray is certain evidence which suggests that the witches sacrificed the god himself—the "divine victim," Frazer's sacred king. The burning of the witches themselves by the public executioner may be understood in many cases as voluntary substitution, sacrifice by surrogate on the part of the worshipers for their god, the cult having presumably reached the point cited by Frazer at which the god is not longer sacrificed in *propria persona*. This is one of the most difficult parts of Murray's doctrine, but she continued to refine it, and presented it in her next book much enlarged, and enriched with examples, among whom were Joan of Arc, Gilles de Rais, William Rufus, and Thomas à Becket.

The organization of the cult, Murray says, was in "as careful a manner as any other religious community; each district however was independent, and therefore Mather is justified in saying that the witches 'form themselves after the manner of Congregational Churches'" (p. 186). The group was properly called a *coven,* and its "'fixed number' among the witches of Great Britain seems to have been thirteen: twelve witches and their officer" (p. 191). Later *(The God of the Witches)* Murray put forward the candidacy of a number of groups celebrated in history for identification as active covens, among them Robin Hood and his merry men.

As to familiars, she distinguishes between two varieties, the divining familiar and the domestic familiar. The place of such minor divinities, or spiritual assistants, in such a cult is obvious: they are relics of a time in which the interdependence of men and animals was vital to survival, and had to be assisted by every possible means.

These were the principal arguments of *The Witch-Cult in Western Europe;* in *The God of the Witches* Murray extended and refined most of them, particularly the suggestion that there was a strong connection between witches and fairies, that in fact they served the same master (as the Church always claimed); that the people who practiced "The cult of the fairy" were actually the witches themselves. There too she elaborated greatly on her theories of the sacred king in connection with witchcraft, as I have mentioned, with special sections on Joan of Arc and the others whom she nominated as "divine victims."

All of Murray's observations were based upon her knowledge of actual cases, some of which indeed seem to lend especial credence to her theories. I should like to mention some half-dozen of these here. A key trial, and a very early one, is that of Lady Alice Kyteler in Kilkenny, Ireland, in 1324. The case is an important one, on several grounds: for one thing, it may be viewed as marking a transitional period between witchcraft as sorcery and the full emergence of the idea of witchcraft as heresy. Then too as the first trial in Ireland it set precedents, including those of torture.

Lady Alice was charged by her bishop (of Ossory, Richard de Ledrede), of holding nightly communion with an evil spirit named Robert Artisson, and sacrificing red cocks to him. She was also supposed to have had sexual relations with the demon, and with him and others of his kind to have blasphemed and denied God and the Church, to have parodied Christian ritual, and have attempted to divine the future. She may actually have been a poisoner: her fourth husband leagued against her with the bishop, to whom he brought some suspicious powders. It is also noteworthy that all of Lady Alice's children except one, who was charged with her, accused her of having poisoned her earlier husbands. After a long struggle with the bishop, the lady proved too powerful to be punished, but she was discredited, and her maid tortured and finally burned, as a gesture to public outrage.

Many aspects of the trial are of particular value to Murray's theories: in particular she cites the sacrifice of the cocks, and Lady Alice's use of a broomstick and flying ointment—a "pipe of ointment" was actually found in her closet (p. 104). The investigators also found there a communion wafer blasphemously altered to fit the worship of the Devil instead of Jesus. The main point, however, is "The Devil, Robert Artisson." Murray returned to the case in *The God of the Witches* with this summation: "In 1324 the Bishop of Ossory tried Dame Alice Kyteler in his ecclesiastical court for the crime of worshipping a deity other than the Christian God" (p. 21). Murray says Dame Alice did not attempt to deny the charges. "Robin," a form of Robert—Robin Artisson, Lady Alice's devil was also called—is a common name for a demon, according to Murray: "Robin Goodfellow"; "Robin Hood."

A much more celebrated case is that of Joan of Arc. Joan had not long been canonized when Murray brought forward considerable evidence, in *The God of the Witches,* that she had in actuality been a leader of the Old Religion, a witch. This reading illuminates many matters hitherto puzzling: the total lack of interest in freeing Joan, for example, on the part of the French, after her capture. This was because she was a Divine Victim whose time for sacrifice had come. Explicable by similar means are Joan's extraordinary persuasive powers and her almost supernatural success at arms: her followers took her to be the incarnate God. Joan's birthplace, Lorraine, was a seedbed of superstitious practices, evidently a center of paganism. Of course Joan's dealings with the fairies, an issue which seems so irrelevant and even foolish to us, was of great significance at the trial, because the authorities knew that witches and fairies were part of the same anti-Christian plot.

The whole trial appears to Murray to have been charactized by an air of deliberate renunciation and self-sacrifice on Joan's part: she was guided by "St. Katherine" (a cult leader), who was present in court; she was offhand and even flippant with her judges; she had said to Charles, "make the most of me, for I shall last only one year." She never mentioned Christ, or even "Our Lord," or "the Savior"; it was always "God," or "my Lord." Finally, her male costume, so often mentioned, had some clear cult significance to her contemporaries: when she put it on again, after having worn woman's dress for a time in prison, "it was the signal for her condemnation. It is possible that the resumption of the dress connoted a resumption of The Old Religion, and that she thereby acknowledged herself a Pagan and the Incarnate God" (p. 190).

This was in the year 1431. In 1440 Gilles de Rais, Joan's chosen companion—of which point Murray makes much—was executed for terrible crimes: sacrilege, sorcery, human sacrifice. Charles Williams re-creates vividly the great moment of the trial—Gilles's reading of his confession (drawn from him by threat of torture) in open court. "In the scene that followed," Williams says, "the whole horror and goodness of the Middle Ages were displayed."

> Gilles began to read. He was dressed in black; his voice was heavy; the confession was full and detailed. The voice continued; murder after murder, pain after pain, loathesomeness after loathesomeness. Once someone screamed. The voice continued: murder after murder, pain after pain, animalism after animalism. The Bishop of Nantes stood up; the voice paused. The bishop went up to the Crucifix that hung over the seats of the judges, and veiled it. There were some things that men could not bear that that carved image should see. The voice broke into repentant cries, to God, to the Church, to the parents of the dead. The bishop came down to the prisoner and embraced him, praying aloud that he might be purged and redeemed. There, clasped, the two stood. That, as well as torture, was the Middle Ages.[3]

The simplest and I think most nearly correct reading of Gilles's case is that it is a classic one of the ennui induced by overwhelming early ingestion of wealth, prestige, and influence—what we, after a famous contemporary autobiography, call "too much too soon." Gilles de Rais was born to vast, almost incalculable wealth; he was the richest noble of his time in Europe. The utter supremacy of his position carried him before long into every sort of wild excess, even to the detriment of his fortune. For a time war occupied his attention, redeemed him, especially Joan's stirring campaigns; but after her death he sank to the depths: child abduction, sexual perversions, and infanticide with every sort of sadistic elaboration. His reckless arrogance eventually embroiled him with the Church and his end was assured. He was tried, condemned, and burned at the stake, mercifully strangled beforehand because of his cooperation. Although skeptics hint at irregularities in the trial, and the political advantages of deflating the overblown nobility (Robbins, p. 407), there seems little doubt that the man had wandered into dark ways. His contemporaries may not have been far off in their judgment of him.

Margaret Murray does point to some curious aspects of the case, the strangest perhaps being the fact that a fountain dedicated on the spot of Gilles's execution, was of especial recourse to nursing mothers; and that children were ritually whipped in remembrance of him. These phenomena and others, she believes, indicate that Gilles, like Joan, was a Divine Victim; to this circumstance also she ascribes the great attention paid to him after sentence, the fact that the bishop and all the people of Nantes walked in his death procession. This sort of conduct she finds otherwise inexplicable, although to Williams, and I think correctly, it is perfectly in the spirit of the Middle Ages.

A case of great importance to the anthropologists, and the most famous trial ever held in Scotland, is that of the North Berwick witches, 1590-92. It presents examples of courage and cruelty, a fantastic plot against a reigning monarch, and introduces to the world of witchcraft a new hero (or villain): James VI of Scotland, the First of England.

The best source for this trial is the contemporary pamphlet, *Newes from Scotland*, which may be found reprinted in the Scottish witchcraft miscellany, *Rowan Tree and Red Thread*.[4] There the emphasis is upon "the damnable life of Doctor Fian, a notable sorcerer, who was burned at Edinburgh, in Januarie last 1591;

which Doctor was Register to The Devill, that sundrie times preached at North Barricks Kirke to a number of notorious witches"; and how this doctor and his hellish crew "pretended [essayed, tried] to bewitch and drowne his Majestie in the sea," and "other wonderfull matters as the like hath not been heard at anie time."[5] Margaret Murray's researches uncovered a plot behind this plot, a serious attempt on the Scottish throne, to be effected by the cult by sorcery as well as physical violence, on behalf of James's near relative Francis Stuart, afterwards Earl of Bothwell, the cult leader as well as next male heir to the throne of Scotland, and England too, if James were to die childless. This Bothwell, nephew and heir to the second husband of Mary Queen of Scots, was indeed known to his contemporaries as a bad lot, a sorcerer and an ambitious malcontent. Murray says he was the Devil—the god—of the cult group in Edinburgh, who appeared to Fian, Agnes Sampson, and the other conspirators, with such lamentable results to them.

According to the view current when Murray formulated this theory, the whole conspiracy was a chimera, a typical burst of hysteria. Notestein's attitude is typical: "It is a story that is easily explained. The confessions were wrung from the supposed conspirators by the various forms of torture 'lately provided for witches in that country'"[6]—tortures which did in fact exceed in barbarity all but the worst excesses of Germany. They are fully given in the old pamphlet. Yet Murray's views so far prevailed that in important studies of the mid-century, the seriousness of the plot, and Bothwell's complicity in it, are taken for granted. Thus Christina Hole in 1945:

> In 1590 A conspiracy against his [James's] life was unmasked in Scotland, of which the leading spirit was no less a person than Francis, Earl of Bothwell, himself a claimant to the Scottish throne should James die without an heir. Unlike the generality of witches, Bothwell really seems to have been a Satanist, or the follower of some dark and obscure creed in which he may himself have been an object of worship.[7]

Pennethorne Hughes, writing in 1952, speaks of "a genuine conspiracy to overthrow James in the interests of Francis, afterwards Earl of Bothwell, who was notoriously addicted to black arts, and who had claims to the throne."[8] Recent scholarship has returned to a more skeptical attitude, as we shall see.

With all this controversy, the trial is an excellent study project for the student. It is full of dramatic moments as well. The best of these was provoked by the king's cross-examination. James was not particularly credulous, in fact decidedly skeptical for the times, but of course deeply concerned with any reports of attempts on his life (poison was mentioned, and the storms that the witches were attempting to raise actually did occur, with spectacular violence). The witches' wilder claims did not impress the king, however. At one point he declared that "they were all extreme lyars":

> Whereat shee [Agnes Sampson] aunswered, "she would not wish his Majestie to suppose her wordes to bee false, but rather to beleve them, in that she would discover such matter unto him as his Majestie should not any way doubt of." And thereupon taking his Majestie a little aside, shee declared unto him the verie words which passed between the Kinges Majestie and his Queene at Upslo in Norway, the first night of mariage, with the answere each to other wherat the Kinges Majestie wondered greatly, and swore "by the living God, that he believed all the divels in hell could not have discovered the same," acknowledging her words to be most true; and therefore gave the more credit to the rest that is before declared.[9]

Parapsychology has an explanation for that sort of phenomenon, but so does witchcraft; we can hardly wonder at our ancestors' response—horror, dismay, and the speedy resort to torture and the stake. The most surprising aspect of the scene is Agnes Sampson's arrogant assertion of her powers, when she was in a fair way to get off; incidentally she was like Fian a person of respectable class. Naturally Murray makes the most of this aspect of the case: Agnes Sampson and Fian were secure in their faith, for which they endured martyrdom which would have done credit to the Christian saints.

A later case in Britain which stirred up enormous excitement was the Lancaster trial of 1612. It is a story of two families living in a remote forest region, steeped in superstition and ancient ways. They quarrelled, and subsequently vied with one another in heaping up accusations of witchcraft. Again there is an important and detailed (though not so easily accessible) pamphlet, *The Wonderful Discovery of Witches in the County of Lancaster* (London, 1613), as well as a good deal of literary reference, the most famous being the play *The Late Lancashire Witches* (London, 1634), by Heywood and Broome.[10]

The assumption among the anthropological party is of course that the genuine cult, the Old Religion, had survived in these areas in something like its ancestral vigor. Christina Hole refers to "what appears to have been a genuine company of witches in Pendle Forest."[11] She is following Murray, whose index in *The Witch-Cult* provides no less than forty-nine citations of the case. Among the many interesting details the trial offers is the appearance of the chief defendants, "Old Demdike" and "Old Chattox," two matriarchal figures of archetypal witchlike age, deformity, and malignity. Old Chattox is described in the pamphlet as "a withered, spent, and decrepit creature"; Demdike as the "rankest hag that ever troubled daylight."[12]

The Lancashire witches behaved for a good part of the time like a conventional gang of outlaws: their "sabbat" consisted of feasting on stolen beef, bacon, and roasted mutton, and they had a plan to rescue their arrested comrades by blowing up Lancaster Castle. Most of the evidence as to their darker purposes seems to have been little better than old gossip, but nevertheless ten of the group were eventually hanged. Naturally, and quite properly, the legality of the evidence is not of so much importance to Murray as its extreme fecundity in significance to her theories. Throughout her books she utilizes it in her discussions of the incarnate god, familiars, sacrifice, and all the details of witch organization and ritual. Incidentally, a witchcraft scare flared up again in the Pendle Forest in 1634, although the authorities are divided as to its relationship to the case of 1612. The anthropological party, like the orthodox, tends to see a continuation, but the skeptics are divided.[13]

One of the principal supports of Murray's hypotheses (seventy references in *Witch-Cult*) is the lengthy deposition of Isobel Gowdie, a witch interrogated in Auldearne, Scotland, in 1662.

Freely and without constraint this woman gave the most particular details of covens as they were allegedly flourishing in Scotland at this period—rites, sacrifices, night-rides, adoration of the devil, feasts, and orgies. Since torture, the skeptics' answer to almost all witchcraft charges, does not figure in the case, Murray's critics find recourse in attacking the informant's sanity, which they do with great indignation: "Unfortunately, on these meanderings of an old woman, two serious scholars, Margaret Murray and Montague Summers, relied to bolster theories of witchcraft no less irrational than Isobel Gowdie's confessions."[14]

All depends on how one reads the evidence. Nowhere is there better illustrated the gulf between the anthropological persuasion and the skeptics than in the case of the Lille witches of 1661. A pious old woman, Madame Bourignon, had founded a home for wayward girls of the lowest classes. After a time she learned that the whole parcel of them, thirty-two girls, were avowed witches, servants of the devil. "As the girls seemed genuinely fond of Madame Bourignon," Margaret Murray writes, "she obtained a considerable amount of information from them,"[15] about the details of the witch cult. From their statements, Murray draws many details about the sexual practices of the pagans. This same case Robbins flatly abandons to humbug: "of many deceptions, possibly the most obvious." The girls "had discovered how to exploit the credulity of Madame Bourignon," and used their revelations as a good way to escape the minor punishments ordained by their softhearted (and softheaded) mentor.[16]

The influence of the anthropological school upon witchcraft studies has been great, both positively and negatively. Important studies, such as Christina Hole's and Pennethorne Hughes's, accepted and incorporated many of Murray's findings. Furthermore, another whole new approach, what I have called the pharmacological, arose partly as a result of her work; certainly it took impetus from her. Almost all the major pharmacological writers are anthropological in outlook, and many if not most of them are actually anthropologists. On the other hand, the dominant school of witchcraft studies, which was and I think remains essentially of the skeptical turn, was roused to take issue with her, and seems to have refuted successfully almost all of her contentions. The full force of the attack upon her came with the publication of her second book, *The God of the Witches*, which is much less tentative than the first, and which promulgates her most controversial doctrines—that Thomas à Becket was a pagan cult leader, for example. The response of the late Julian Franklyn may be taken as typical: "In 1933,[17] Dr. Margaret Murray published a book entitled *The God of the Witches*. All who admired her as an Egyptologist and folklorist of outstanding merit were saddened by this publication because in it Miss Murray had bent the facts to fit the theory."[18]

One of the first, and one of the most cogent, attacks on Murray's theories appeared in 1933, in *Witchcraft and Demonianism* by C. L'Estrange Ewen, who brought forth strong evidence against the very existence of the "coven," the formal group of thirteen. He also attributed much of the trial revelations to torture and drugs. Writing in 1938, George Lincoln Burr magisterially dismissed Murray along with her theories: "her training was not that of the historian, and she seems to have felt it needless to equip herself by a knowledge of what has been written by historians."[19]

Elliott Rose in 1962 took time to consider Murray's theory in detail, and demolished it.[20] More recent studies have been dismissive—Keith Thomas's *Religion and the Decline of Magic* (1971); Alan Macfarlane's *Witchcraft in Tudor and Stuart England* (1971)—and in other cases, punishing. Norman Cohn, for example, whom we have had occasion to cite repeatedly as one of the most impressive scholars currently in the field, is particularly damaging because he demonstrates that Margaret Murray *edited* her material so as to emphasize its matter-of-fact aspects—her account of the Lancashire gang, for example—while suppressing the fantastic. "Stories which have manifestly impossible features," he observes, "are not to be trusted in any particular, as evidence of what physically happened" (*Europe's Inner Demons*, p. 115). In attacking her cases he is indeed laying the axe to the roots; his views of the Kyteler case emphasize the feuding among various stepchildren for the family inheritance, and are I think persuasive. Family feuding is also a prominent feature of the Salem trials, dealt with below.

Cohn goes further in his charges, to attack those who seem to support Murray, among them Jeffrey Russell. Russell, for all his erudition, seems to me at times to waffle on the issue of the survival of pagan cults; but he is clearly no Murray follower. He too finds her use of sources "appalling" *(Witchcraft in the Middle Ages,* p. 37), and eliminates the possibility of the existence of a formal witch cult, "the quantity (not quality) or Murrayite and occulist [*sic*] assertion to the contrary . . ." (p. 22).[21] Only among the pharmacologists does Murray's name still shine; the idea of an anti-establishment, drug-consuming cult is gratifying to them, as to numbers of the transcendentalists and occultists who make much of the witchcraft news today. The truth would seem to be that fragments of pre-Christian belief, preserved in confused state in the popular mind, did certainly survive in Europe long past the "Dark" or "Middle Ages," and unquestionably survive there still. The concept of an organized pre- and anti-Christian religious force, however, seems to have been engendered in the twilit fancies of the Christian establishment itself; the very charges leveled at "witches" had proven serviceable against scores of earlier heretics. The overabundance of sexual material embedded in these charges is less likely to have risen from surviving fertility cults than from the tremendous force of the sexual repression created and maintained by the dominant moral code.

That is not to say that Margaret Murray's findings should be tossed out as totally useless. Like the eighteenth-century poet and antiquarian James Macpherson, who claimed to have discovered in *Ossian* a finished Celtic epic, Murray, though with nothing of Macpherson's duplicity, may be thought of as one whose enthusiasms led her from some notable discoveries to an ultimately untenable position. But Macpherson was a poet of genius, however one cares to take his theories; and Murray, whether one grants her premises or not, must be thought of as an original and fascinating writer, one who reinvigorated her field of study in a way that very few scholars have ever succeeded in doing. The kindest summation may be Kieckhefer's: ". . . it is conceivable that anti-authoritarian, devil-worshipping assemblies may have taken place. Their occurrence is not demonstrable, but it is conceivable" *(European Witch Trials,* p. 42).

7.The Psychological School

A position at once old and honorable, is that many if not most of the participants in the great witchcraft persecutions were out of their minds. First, as we noted, there is an old skeptical tradition, which forms the basis of such official pronouncements as the *Canon Episcopi*, to the effect that all the paraphernalia of witchcraft is delusion. Whatever the witches thought they did or saw, the fact is that those deeds and sights proceeded from their own disordered imaginations. The second part of the theory is that delusion took an early grip upon the authorities as well, the witch-persecutors, so that they soon became as astray in their wits as their victims. The spectacle of the trials attracted all sorts of sadists, voyeurs, and perverts, to both sides. The ravings of the witches were matched by the unleashed fantasies and special cruelties of the inquisitors.

Another theory is that some phenomena actually did occur which are inexplicable in conventional scientific terms. It is now possible to see these occurrences, such as poltergeist outbreaks, or Agnes Sampson's revelations to King James, as the effects of natural forces still poorly understood: telepathy, telekinesis, extrasensory perception. These phenomena are now usually considered to be generated by the brain, in accordance with principles concerning which there is wide disagreement. This area of study, which looks to become extremely fruitful in another few years, is generally called parapsychology.

Delaying entrance into this disputed territory for a time, we might begin with the consideration of the psychology of the witch versus the psychology of the witch-hunter. And we find that, in some ways, the two are much alike. A key element in both is the sexual, expressed, in the case of the witches (their alleged fertility rites, orgies, sex crimes, etc.), and repressed on the part of the witch-hunters (fantasies, voyeurism, torture). I don't think it farfetched to consider these as predictably varying responses to the sexual urge, in a society which spends much of its time and energy crushing that urge. Sex would be of interest to men, we may assume, even if it did not carry the weight of religious inhibition, state regulation, myth and symbol which has been loaded upon it in our culture. As it is, sex has for long ages been invested with a double fascination, that of mystery and illegality in addition to its own native attraction.

At the center of the repression was the considerable antisexual and antifeminine bias of the Church itself. Christ's own attitude toward women is still much debated, but a clear antifeminine trend emerges with Paul and the early Fathers, some of whom, especially the so-called Desert Saints, were vouchsafed demonic visions of a decidedly female character. The trend was emphasized by the decision for clerical celibacy, and the development of a mythos around great female culprits of the Old Testament like Eve and Jezebel. These of course were inheritances from the decidedly patriarchal Jews, but the Christians elaborated upon the material. The countercurrent (and to feminists no doubt even more odious) was the enormous cult of the Virgin Mary, which supplied the churchmen with a satisfactorily inhuman and unapproachable model of female virtue. The ordinary, earthbound woman was a shoddy work, decidedly an afterthought of the Creator and correspondingly ill-designed. Her spiritual and moral incapacity, combined with dubious physical attractions, made her Satan's chief avenue of entrance into the world of men. If anyone thinks this too strong a statement, let him look back at the *Malleus Maleficarum* in chapter 4, and its "feminus = fe-minus." "All witchcraft comes from carnal lust," says the *Malleus*, "which is in women insatiable."

The sexual offenses of the witches were many. First of all they were accused of promiscuous sexual intercourse with each other, of orgies; and also of ritual marriages unhallowed by the Church. Furthermore they were accused of homosexual practices and perversions of all sorts. Still worse, they were said to welcome relations with demons, even with Satan himself, which amounted of course to bestiality, since demons were of a different species. We have all heard of the incubus devils who persecute women with their attentions; these demons sought out not only the ungodly but also the most pious of women; they even entered the cells of the saints. It is almost universally accepted now that the incubus and its female counterpart, the succubus (of whom, typically, we hear much less, men supposedly being less lecherous) represent a primitive explanation of certain aspects of normal sexual development in men and women, as erotic dreams, and nocturnal emissions. Our ancestors were however sorely puzzled by these phenomena. They spent years of their lives developing theories to explain them. Does the demon actually take a human form during these visitations? If so, whose? Is semen emitted? Where does it come from? Can children be born of these unions? *That* gave play to the Gothic imagination. We have already noted Guazzo at work on these problems; most of the classic demonologists investigated them thoroughly.

By the time that the sabbat with all its details had become received opinion, witches were expected to confess to sexual enormities, and all too often, were tortured until they did. The fantasy of the inquisitors meanwhile reached new heights: they discovered among other things that a certain type of devil had been developed with a double and even a triple penis, so that he might abuse his victims, and, presumably, please his devotees, at more than one orifice simultaneously.[1]

This sort of activity differed from *possession*, a state which may be said to exist when a demon or "unclean spirit," to use the New Testament terminology, actually inhabits his victim. There are however markedly sexual aspects of this state as well. Under the influence of the possessing demon, the victim, usually a woman, indulges typically in the most uninhibited behavior, shrieking obscenities, contorting her body into provocative attitudes, and often engaging in frenzied autoerotic activity. Naturally this behavior excites great interest in the community, and the Church's complex ritual of exorcism usually tends only to aggravate the symptoms, at least during the early period of the affliction, which may go on for years. Of course the attention of the exorcism is the desired result of the possession. Like the child who is always being punished, the victim of psychic invasion has managed to make herself the center of attention.

To be sure, the personality displacement of the victim, often coupled with striking parapsychological manifestations such as thought transference, has a devastating effect on the bystanders, and upon the exorcists, who sometimes themselves go mad, sicken, or actually die. The classic text on the subject is T.K. Oesterreich's *Possession*, published in German in 1921, and still in print I believe in a recent English edition (New Hyde Park, New York: University Books, 1966). Robbins also has an excellent entry, and there are a number of articles in the Jesus-Marie anthology *Satan* mentioned earlier. The phenomenon is by no means restricted to the Western world; on the contrary it is very common throughout Asia.[2] Whatever help our psychology may offer us in understanding it, it terrified our ancestors, and was to them one of the most conclusive proofs of the activity of the Devil among them.

Though accused of engaging in constant sexual activity, witches were often blamed for inhibiting the sexual function. This hellish art, technically known as ligature, was one of the sorcerer's most feared powers. Because impotence so often occurs for no obvious reason, but rather at moments apparently the most auspicious of success, like wedding nights, sixteenth-century people were the more ready to ascribe it to devil's work. The standard procedure was to introduce by some means into the victim's possession a knotted string, tied up with the most formidable charms. Of course, the very sight of such a device was usually enough to render a nervous bridegroom incapable.

Thence mystic knots make great abuse
On young guidmen, fond, keen, an' croose;
When the best wark-lume i' the house
    By cantraip wit,
Is instant made no worth a louse,
    Just at the bit.[3]

"Just at the bit" may be translated as "just when the need is greatest." The "guidman" is of course the groom, the newly married man.[4]

Burns is of course writing well past the great days of the belief; fortunately we have another witness to call, a sixteenth-century one, and of all men the one we should most like to examine on any doubtful subject. Montaigne's good sense and decency have kept him bright in men's memories to the present day. Although he might admire Bodin's literary gifts (and by a curious coincidence his grandniece married de Lancre), he would have nothing to do with the witch-hunting mania. "After all," he writes, "it is setting a very high price on one's conjectures to burn a man alive for them."[5]

Montaigne was essentially a skeptic, although not a hardened one. His famous motto, "what do I know?" indicates that he was not the sort to dismiss all stories of the supernatural as simple absurdities. "The more I know of myself," he says, "the less I understand."[6] His observations of the hysteria all around him mark him as an amateur psychologist of distinction. He has several stories of ligature, "those amusing spells which occupy our age—we hardly talk of anything else—" and writes them down as "the result of apprehension and fear." In one episode he himself played a major role. A good friend, on the eve of his wedding, feared magical reprisals from a disappointed suitor. Montaigne assured him that he had ready a counter-charm of absolutely certain efficacy; and when the crucial moment came, with the groom "thwarted by his troubled imagination," he stepped forward with the amulet, accompanied by a lot of mumbo-jumbo, and the issue was triumphantly resolved. "These monkey tricks are essential to success," he sums up.[7]

One other aspect of witchcraft seems implicitly, if not directly, sexual. This is the "Evil Eye"—"fascination," "mal occhio," "glamour," or whatever else it is called all over the world. This ancient folk-belief was early assimilated along with many others into the witchcraft canon. What is not generally recognized, however, is the sexual nature of this superstition. The charm against it is "generally a phallus," as Robbins remarks;[8] what he might have added is a comment on the sexual significance of the eye itself, an ancient female symbol. "The Evil Eye" may be a sublimated expression of a very primitive anxiety, indeed: the blind basic male fear of extinction in the vagina (in the sex act).[9]

The werewolf and the vampire too are susceptible to psychological explanation. They are not the principal subjects of this essay, but may not be entirely omitted from it, largely because of the success of orthodox theory in identifying them with the Satanic plot. Montague Summers has a solid book on each, *The Vampire* (New York, 1929), and *The Werewolf* (London, 1933), which sum up the traditional view as well as any inquisitor could wish. More congenial to the present time is Ornella Volta's brilliant monograph, *The Vampire*, of which there is an English translation available in paperback (London, 1965). This is so far the definitive study; Volta combines masterful intuition with thorough knowledge of the sources, historical, anthropological, mythical, and more particularly sexological and psychopathological.

An earlier, similarly ambitious project on behalf of the werewolf was undertaken by John Eisler: *Man Into Wolf / an Anthropological Interpretation of Sadism, Masochism and Lycanthropy* (New York, 1952). This heavily annotated work is not convincing, largely because of its author's eccentric forays into the realms of vegetarianism and pacificism, but it brings together under its covers much important material, and is well worth consultation. William Seabrook's *Witchcraft / Its Power in the World Today* (New York, 1940) has many excellent firsthand accounts of witchcraft, vampire, and werewolf phenomena. Seabrook is a first-rate observer, honest and very open; he tends towards a psychological view of the incidents he records.

Of course the classical school of psychoanalysis showed interest in these phenomena; we might mention two important studies: the first, by Freud himself, is that popularly known as "the Wolf Man" (Freud called it "The History of an Infantile Neurosis"); it may be found printed in the volume *Three Case Histories*, in the *Collier Collected Papers of Sigmund Freud* (New York, 1963). Briefly, Freud found that his patient's incapacitating wolf-obsession was the result of unconscious fears of his father. The second study is Ernest Jones's *On the Nightmare* (London, 1931). Here Jones comments upon the psychological importance of an embodied principle of evil; the Devil derives both from our wish to imitate the father, and our need to defy him.

The witches, then, and all the beliefs popularly associated with them, are fit subjects for psychological speculation. But what of the witch-hunters, who so enjoyed their duties of receiving confessions and administering torture? In this connection one is struck by a remark by Boguet: he wished that all witches might "be united in one single body, so that they might all be burned at once in a single fire."[10] If that remark sounds familiar, the reader may want to consult Suetonius, where he will find almost the same sentiments ascribed to the emperor Caligula.[11] There is no need to belabor the point, much less to bring in Robbins's overwhelming data on means, varieties, and duration of torture at the trials; it is enough to say that the witch-persecutions, like all persecutions, brought to the surface in people some very sinister elements; and it brought to the surface of society some people who might, if these opportunities had been lacking, been forced themselves into crime in order to act out their desires.

The trials are rich in psychological data. One thinks at once of the many nunnery scandals, most of them in France. Nuns were particularly tempting to the Devil. The most famous of these cases is the trial of Urbain Grandier in Loudun in 1633-34. Because the matter was taken up recently by a major author, Aldous Huxley, in *The Devils of Loudun* (London, 1952), the facts are readily available to the student. It is the familiar story of a high-living clergyman brought down by a political conspiracy under cover of witchcraft charges. Father Grandier's connections had brought him safely out of the well-founded charges of immorality against him, but not out of the disfavor of Richelieu, whom he had been foolish enough to insult. The charges against Grandier seem to have been completely fabricated, the court irregularly constituted, and the trial a mockery. Favorable witnesses, of whom there were many, were brutally intimidated and forced in most cases to flee for their lives. Favorable evidence was suppressed, and nuns penitent at having borne false witness against the prisoner were ignored. Grandier was tortured until the marrow oozed from his bones, but would confess nothing, even though a document purporting to be his actual pact with the Devil was circulated in court (this has been widely reprinted in such source books as Robbins's *Encyclopedia* and Seligmann's *History of Magic* [New York, 1948]). He was eventually burned alive.

More to our purpose here is the scandalous behavior of the possessed nuns, who were by no means quieted at Grandier's death. Their bodily contortions were frightful: "one, the Mother Superior, stretched her legs to such an extraordinary extent that, from toe to toe, the distance was seven feet, though she herself was but four feet high."[12] "One is forced to the conclusion," Huxley adds, "that, as well as *naturaliter Christiana*, the feminine soul is *naturaliter Drum-Majoretta.*"[13] The nuns also used expressions "so filthy as to shame the most debauched of men, while their acts, both in exposing themselves and in inviting lewd behavior from those present would have astounded the inhabitants of the lowest brothel in the country."[14] After Grandier's death the prioress actually went through an hysterical pregnancy, complete with morning sickness, secretion of milk, and "a marked enlargement of the belly." Still another miracle of Hell, and eventually so revealed during a large public exorcism, when the sister vomited the whole business out in blood.

The psychological consequences of Grandier's inhuman persecution upon his persecutors, were themselves remarkable. Infected by the vicious hate, the sickness, the violence, many of the most prominent among them did not live long after their victim. The exorcist Father Lactance died screaming and cursing just one month after Grandier, tormented by legions of devils. Mannoury the surgeon saw a vision of the dead Grandier, fell to the ground, and died within a week. Chauvet, an honest judge who had deplored the proceedings, passed from depression to madness and death. Father Tranquille, one of Grandier's most persistent enemies, caught all the nun's worst symptoms, and died "vomiting filths and stinks so insupportable, that his attendants had to throw them out without delay, so fearfully was the room infected by them."[15]

The data from these unpleasant proceedings may be enlarged by study of any number of similar cases. Robbins has entered in his *Encyclopedia* (pp. 229, 301) an account of the late Victorian incident of Louise Lateau, the "Belgian Stigmatic." Her ecstatic state induced in her spontaneous bleeding, that which taking the form of the wounds of Christ is called the stigmata, as well as typical frenzied behavior: contortion, choking, convulsions, weeping, rigidity, etc. "Because she lived in the second half of the nineteenth century, however," Robbins notes, "her condition was recorded by medical men rather than by demonologists or exorcists." Her symptoms may be compared to the hystero-epileptic fits of Sister Jeanne Fery who, living in Mons three hundred earlier, was treated to some twelve years' attention by exorcists.[16] The clear conclusion is, that exorcism in most cases is no cure, but an extension of the malady. The best way to cure a possessed person is to ignore him completely.

The last witchcraft trial in England suggests alternative methods: the chief witness for the prosecution was Anne Thorne, a young servant girl who was tormented by fits and visions of devils. "A doctor ordered her to wash her hands and face twice a day, and to be watched by a 'lusty young fellow' during her convalescence. The young man proved an effective cure for Anne's hysterics, and the two were happily married."[17]

Possession has by no means ceased in our time, either. Oesterreich notes that possessing agents are now more likely to be spirits of the departed rather than demons; see in this connection the voluminous lore of spiritualism. A most helpful new summary of much of this data may be found in Robert Somerlott's *Here Mr. Splitfoot / An Informal Exploration into Modern Occultism* (New York, 1971). Recently I came across a sensational but now forgotten case in the pages of the *Cornhill Magazine*, for April 1865 (11, pp. 468 ff), called "The Devils of Morzine." This account tells of the gradual bewitchment of a whole town in mid-nineteenth-century Savoy. Possessed citizens displayed fantastic muscular strength and dexterity; one small boy rushed in his frenzy up an enormous tree and then couldn't get back down, until his brother prayed for the devil to enter him again, when he scuttled down headfirst like a squirrel. Attempts at exorcism as usual only made things worse; frail housewives, full of demonic power, tossed gendarmes about like straws. France, which had recently annexed Savoy, was greatly embarrassed by these disorders; eventually the only means she found to arrest them was to clear out the whole area, take the possessed villagers away from each other, and carry them off to widely separate regions. This did the trick. The hysteria, it seems clear, was religious in origin.

My own favorite witchcraft case is that of Major Thomas Weir of Edinburgh in 1670, which I first ran across in Summers, who calls it "one of the most astounding and terrible cases in the whole annals of Scottish Witchcraft." And, perhaps, of witchcraft in general: the extensive account in Summers's *Geography* (pp. 231-44), which quotes contemporary sources, is still the best readily available. Major Weir, an absolute pillar of the community and model of rectitude, startled all Edinburgh by confessing, in the seventieth year of his age, that he had for many years practiced in secret "crimes of the most revolting nature." At first no one would believe him—a woman who had once accused him of irregularities was herself whipped by the common hangman as a slanderer of the godly—but after a time his story compelled belief and he was jailed. Even then the authorities were most ready to believe that his mind had given way, but doctors who examined him assured the provost that "the Major was in good health." They believed that "his distemper was only an ulcerated conscience."

Weir had been an example of piety even among the saints. A devout and intemperate Presbyterian, he had been zealous in suppressing the Papists (which explains Summers's special animus against him); furthermore "He could not so much as endure to look upon an Orthodox [Anglican] Minister; but when he met any of them in the street, he would pull his hat over his eyes in a pharisaical kind of indignation and contempt." While commander of the Guards of the City of Edinburgh in 1649-50, he behaved with "great cruelty and insolence towards the Loyal party [the Cavaliers]." In particular, according to Summers's sources, he rejoiced over them as they were led out to public execution.

This behavior, as Summers well notes, "passed among the people for extraordinary zeal," and Major Weir became an important community leader. He was particularly well served by his extreme piety; people would come from fifty miles to hear him pray. But he would not preach, for fear of offending the Kirk. Nevertheless his prayers were entertainment enough; during them he carried on with such raptures and ecstasies "that he appeared transported." He took to visiting people for the purposes of prayer and exhortation; "and it was his practice to visit married women at such times especially as their husbands were from home."

Scott, who pays some notice to the case in his *Letters On Demonology and Witchcraft*, comments, "It appears that the Major, with a maiden sister who kept his house, was subject to fits of melancholic lunacy, an infirmity easily reconcilable with the formal pretences which he made to a high show of religious zeal" (p. 265).

One of the more curious aspects of the case is that the Major depended upon the efficacy of a charmed stick "of peculiar shape and appearance"; unless he had it in his hand "he could not pray with the same warmth and fluency of expression." "It was noticed, in short, that when his stick was taken from him, his wit and talent seemed to forsake him" (Scott, p. 265). This staff was taken from the prisoner by the arresting officers on the advice of his sister (and codefendant):

> "When they were seized, she desired the guards to keep him from laying hold on a certain staff, which, she said, if he chanced to get into his hands he would certainly drive them all out of doors, notwithstanding all the resistance they could make." This magical staff was all of one piece, with a crooked head of thornwood. She said he received it of the Devil, and did many wonderful things with it, particularly that he used to lean upon it in his hypocritical prayers.[18]

The importance of this fetish to the prisoner has also interested the anthropological school: although Weir may have been insane, "it is clear that he had a considerable knowledge of magic and he may have practiced it as he said."[19] That the sister was mad, almost no one doubts. She told the authorities a rambling, self-contradictory tale of commerce with the "Queen of Farie," traffic with the Devil, and keeping a familiar spirit, as well as all sorts of sexual irregularities. For the main charges against the Major, upon his own recommendation, let it be remembered, were sexual. He had never married, but had committed incest with his sister since their childhood (she was not much younger than he), as well as fornication with a number of other women, and bestiality with a cow and with his own riding-mare. These were the counts on which the Major was actually found guilty, and for which he was burned alive. His sister was hanged; at the scaffold she combined religious harangues with efforts to "cast off all hir cloths before all the multitude."

The Major's behavior in prison has drawn much comment, in his day and after. When "some charitable ministers of the city" offered to pray with him, he first attempted to interrupt them, and failing in that, gave himself over to a "stupid" and resigned attitude. He steadfastly denied that any efforts on his behalf could do him any good.

To what extent did Thomas Weir actually practice upon his community over some fifty years, and to what extent were all his crimes acted out only in his own mind? This is not an easy question. Lea says, "The general modern opinion is that he was insane."[20] True enough; in this case I prefer to take my stand with the thoughtful and humane Charles Williams, who can come only to this indistinct conclusion: "The Weir case began with the interior distress of Thomas Weir—whether he had actually committed the deeds he declared or whether his unbalanced mind did but brood on the dreams till he thought they were facts."[21] No one will ever know the truth now, beyond that the man did most certainly go through a terrible psychic agony.

When we come to the field of parapsychology we are on uncertain ground indeed. *Did* the old trials document—and even produce—data which really is "supernatural," or as we might say, beyond the capacity of conventional science to measure? Can such phenomena exist? Certainly the word "supernatural" at least is a contradiction, and an embarrassing one which deters much serious investigation. Whatever exists, cannot be "supernatural." We probably ought to begin by introducing Professor J. B. Rhine, the famous psychic investigator. His is the most prestigious name in a field which academia believes, perhaps rightly, to be crowded with quacks—and even he, with all his years of controlled experiments, has not been able to convince everyone, or even I think the majority of the scientific community.

Rhine's studies are somewhat peripheral to our concerns here, but they may be seen as laying foundations for investigation of any branch of what is called the "occult." What Rhine has been after, and succeeded in proving to the satisfaction of many, may be simply stated. "We have found," he writes, "that there is a capacity for acquiring knowledge that transcends the sensory functions."[22] Beyond that, he has courageously ventured to the edge, at least, of the field of metaphysics: does the human personality survive death?

Can we find "an effective morality," with or without proof of a soul, for our ethically confused world? He has no answer ready, but even to ask such questions makes a man suspect in the twentieth-century scientific world, just as to ignore them would have made the seventeenth-century scientist a candidate for burning. Rhine's major works are available in Apollo paperbacks: *The Reach of the Mind* (1968, originally 1947), quoted above, and *New World of the Mind* (1968, originally 1953).

A book which monitors Rhine's achievements, as well as those of Leonard Vasiliev of Leningrad, is *ESP: A Scientific Evaluation,* by C. E. M. Hansel (New York: Scribners, 1966). Hansel is a severe critic; he admits that some evidence for ESP exists, but doubts that it can ever be definitively proven in the laboratory. Space programs, both American and Russian, have given new impetus to experiments in ESP: see Sheila Ostrander and Lynn Schroeder, *Psychic Discoveries Behind the Iron Curtain* (New York: Bantam Books, 1971). An excellent collection of studies, some of them however now out of date, is George Devereux's *Psychoanalysis and the Occult* (New York, n.d.). Here the student may find Freud's six principal statements on such matters as telepathy and occult significance of dreams, along with a whole string of studies, some of them "pioneering"—as those by Edward Hitschmann—and some "new"—these would be findings of the early fifties.

The material is thus somewhat dated, and written in none of the liveliest style (the scholarly paper is its model), but it remains a first-rate source book, especially because of its careful organization and fine bibliography (204 items). One of the contributors to it, Nandor Fodor, has actually turned his attention to our subjects of witchcraft, lycanthropy, and vampirism.

Fodor resembles Seabrook in many ways, although he operates from a professional rather than an amateur base. But both men share a disarming willingness to suspend judgment, a determination to be honest, despite embarrassment, and the capacity for ranging far and wide in search of the rare, the strange, the bizarre in human life. Fodor like Seabrook has been much in the company of spiritualists, healers, gurus, unorthodox divines, sorcerers and psychopaths, which gives the timid an excellent reason to discount his observations; but the disinterested reader will probably find him a more congenial companion than most of the researchers into these subjects.

His first major contribution was in the study of the poltergeist. As early as 1948 Fodor was speaking of "poltergeist psychosis," in an article in the *Psychiatric Quarterly* (April 1948), since reprinted in his important text *Haunted People*, a casebook of poltergeist incidents compiled with Hereward Carrington (New York, 1951). He had begun to formulate his theories in the thirties while investigating poltergeist cases for the International Institute of Psychic Research. ". . . it became clear to me that the basis of the disturbance was not to be found in any discarnate spirit, but rather in Mrs. Forbes' own mind and personality."[23]

This sort of finding was displeasing to the society, and a battle followed, during the course of which Fodor appealed to Freud for support. The master was sympathetic, even admiring, and Fodor's course was set. Later findings confirmed him in his belief that the poltergeist was the manifestation of a troubled mental state, usually of a youth at the onset of puberty. He presented his findings in *On The Track of The Poltergeist* (New York, 1958), indubitably the most considerable study ever published on this troublesome subject. The next year he brought out his memoirs under the title *The Haunted Mind*, with many fascinating additional episodes from his long psychiatric practice. Here he goes over his earlier poltergeist findings once more, posing the original questions: "can the human psyche operate outside the periphery of the body? Is psychokinesis or telekinesis . . . . really possible? Is there some connection between the newly-forming sexual powers of the youngster in puberty and the outbreak of this strange force? Is such a manifestation to be viewed as a cry for therapy and does it accomplish a form of self-therapy when the disturbance ceases of its own accord, as it so often does?"(p. 49). There is still no definite answer, he concludes, but we are making progress into these mysteries. In the meantime he has continued to revise his earlier hypotheses: poltergeist phenomena are not invariably associated with the presence of a youth, but may be triggered by an older person with unresolved youthful anxieties.

In his capacities as psychoanalyst and psychic investigator, Fodor came upon dozens of sensational "supernatural" episodes; in fact he made a reputation as a notable debunker of frauds in these areas. He is of most interest to the present study however when describing vampire and werewolf phenomena which he has clearly traced to psychoses. One of his most brilliant cures involved a haunting, concerning which his principle may be roughly paraphrased thus: happy people are not haunted. Subject the victims of persistent haunting to psychotherapy or analysis, and you may turn up deep personal problems which can actually manifest themselves physically. Fodor told one such woman that "she had been wasting her vitality in a vain attempt to convey a message, in the same way neurotic symptoms manifest themselves" (p. 66). Elsewhere, concluding the account of a case, he remarks,

> The psychologist or psychoanalyst might say that the final revelations pointed clearly to the fact that the ghost was a pure invention of Mr. Keel's subconscious. However, the psychical researcher has a right to wonder if there was not, at some time in the beginning, an occurrence that was truly para-normal in character. It may be that those who put themselves in an unguarded psychological position, in a place filled with historical memories and traditions do, on rare occasions, come into contact with a force or an intelligence other than their own. (P. 115)

That I think is the place to end this chapter, before it intrudes upon matters which we call the occult. But even the most orthodox studies of the human consciousness have a tendency to carry us far from safe ground, downward into strange realms, as Aldous Huxley puts it,[24]

> Down into convulsions; down into swinish squalor or maniacal rage. Down, far down, below the level of personality, into that sub-human world, in which it seemed natural for an aristocrat to play tricks for the amusement of the mob, for a nun to blaspheme and strike indecent postures and

shout unmentionable words. And then down, still further, down into stupor, down into catalepsy, down into the ultimate bliss of total unconsciousness, of absolute and complete oblivion.

8. The Pharmacological School: Witchcraft and Drugs

In the early days of witchcraft investigations, no one doubted that the powerful drugs which the witches applied liberally to themselves and to others, were the cause of many if not most of the bizarre phenomena reported. A typical story, and a famous one, is that told by Johannes Nider: a certain woman undertook to prove to her confessor, a Dominican, that she actually could fly through the air with Diana. He was present, along with other witnesses, when she anointed herself with the magic oil, while sitting in a large mixing bowl, or kneading trough, which had been placed on a bench. After uttering appropriate incantations she fell into a drugged sleep, during which she tossed about so violently as to throw herself and the bowl off the bench, so that she injured herself severely. The Dominican, by appealing to the other witnesses, was able to convince her that her experiences were delusions, the result of the poisons she had administered to herself.[1]

Giambattista Porta had a similar experience: while he was mulling over the wild tales current about sabbats and night flights, there fell into his hands an old woman who readily confessed that she had participated in such activities, and offered to fly off and bring him evidence, news from afar. She withdrew into a private room, but Porta and his friends were able to observe her through the cracks in the door. They saw her strip naked, anoint herself, and fall asleep. Nothing they could do could wake her; they even beat her. When she woke up she told of a wild flight over mountains and seas, but her news was not convincing. They were not able to persuade her that she had never left the room, even when they showed her the bruises they had given her.[2]

It seems that such oils and potions were in use. Paulus Grillandus saw and handled them, unguents used to poison men and animals, and another which caused insanity. He ordered them burnt.[3] But as the witch enthusiasm blazed more furiously, men's attention was drawn from mundane oils and salves to spiritual questions. We have seen how the corporeal reality of the sabbat and all its horrors came to be articles of faith for the good Christian. Rational explanations were not popular during the great witch-hunts. Then in the cold morning light of the eighteenth century, witches' ointments were chucked out along with all the rest of the phantasmagoria. It was left to the late nineteenth, and much more significantly, the twentieth century, to resume serious inquiry into the witches' pharmacopoeia.

A Dr. Otto Snell, a German, was experimenting with witches' ointments in the late 1880's with no glamorous results. Instead of erotic fantasies, he got a headache. His conclusions were that, to get the effects they reported, the witches must have used potions of a toxicity which would preclude frequent use.[4] Other early experiments were similarly cautious. A Dr. Robert Fletcher in 1896 presented to the Johns Hopkins Hospital Historical Club a lengthy paper on the witches pharmacopoeia. A compendium of literary erudition, folklore, and late Victorian medical science (the toad's venom "if it have any"), it is almost totally useless to us, except for some curious remarks on the use of parsley.[5] A. J. Clark, in 1921, observed that rubbing drugs into the skin is not an efficient way of introducing them into the body. He added however that a "medieval witch's skin" was not likely to be unbroken. Furthermore if an ointment is rubbed into the skin in sufficient quantities, "definite physiological results would be produced."

Clark gives three formulae for flying ointment: the first, of parsley, water of aconite, poplar leaves and soot; the second, water parsnip, sweet flag, cinquefoil, bat's blood, deadly nightshade, and oil; the third, baby's fat, juice of water parsnip, aconite, cinquefoil, deadly nightshade, and soot.

> These prescriptions show [he says] that the society of
> witches had a very creditable knowledge of the art of
> poisoning: aconite and deadly nightshade or belladonna are
> two of the three most poisonous plants growing freely in
> Europe, the third is hemlock, and in all probability "persil"
> refers to hemlock and not to the harmless parsley which it
> resembles closely.

Clark also thinks that the "water parsnip" specified may actually
have been "the poisonous water hemlock or cowbane. The baby's
fat and bat's blood would of course have no action."[6]

It is worth jumping ahead of ourselves just long enough to
observe that along with all the other new insights which our time
has provided into the nature of drugs, it has even brought suspicion
to the baby fat. Although we have noted that child murder and
cannibalism were stock charges against minority groups, present
medical opinion sees an important role for *some* fatty substance in
these drugs. Fat provides an occlusive dressing which greatly
enhances the absorption of any medication on the skin.[7]

Clark will not commit himself to the theory that the potions he
studied would "produce the impression of flying," but he does
consider the aconite "interesting in this respect." He also suggests
"mental confusion" and "irregular action of the heart" as
consequences of the drugs.[8] Dr. H. J. Norman, who contributed an
appendix on ointments to Summers's *The Werewolf* in 1933, was
also suggestive, but careful.

"It is not an easy matter to decide what the effects of these,
frequently complicated, concoctions may have been," he begins.
He grants the absorption of the drugs through the skin, but thinks
it unlikely that the resultant concentration of the drugs in the
system would have been of significant strength. "The chief effect
was brought about," he writes, "as a result of the high degree of
suggestibility of the individuals, who were undoubtedly in
numerous instances psychopathic and mentally deranged."[9]

At this point, two questions. We have ascertained that the
witches did use unguents, and that numerous half-hearted attempts
were made to determine their effect. The student has a right to
inquire first, whether we know what was actually in these potions,

and how we know; and secondly, whether we have any real evidence of the effects of such substances on the human body. To answer the latter question, we are now provided with a wealth of information made commonly available just within the last few years; to answer the former, we must go back to the days of the witch-hunts themselves.

We know what the witches used in their unguents because the witches themselves told people, often without constraint, and the old chroniclers who occupied so much of our time in chapter 5 reproduced the recipes faithfully in their texts. The student today will find much of this material in the source books so often referred to here. Summers, for instance, spends a great deal of his time on *The Werewolf* citing old unguent recipes. In his chapter 2, concerned with the werewolf's "science and practice," Summers quotes Jean de Nynauld[10] as to the witches' ointments:

> la racin de la belladonna, morelle furieuse, sang de chauve sourris, d'huppe, l'aconit, la berle, la morelle endormante, l'ache, la saye, le pentaphilon, l'acorum vulgaire, le persil, feuilles du peuplier, l'opium, l'hyoscyame, cyguë, les especes de pauot, l'hyuroye, le *synochytides*, qui fait voir les ombres des Enfers, c. d. les mauvais espirits, comme au contraire, l' *Anachitides* faict apparoit les images des saincts anges. (P. 98)

The reader will recognize aconite and belladonna; "morelle" is deadly nightshade; "sang de chauve sourris" is bat's blood. "L'ache" is sweet flag; "Saye" may mean "suye," soot, a common ingredient. Most by these items we have already noticed in A. J. Clark, who in fact seems to have lifted his list directly from the skeptic Johan Weyer. Especially noteworthy in Nynauld's list are opium and henbane ("hyoscyame"). "Berle" and "ache" may refer to species of hemlock, as may "persil," as Clark observes. "Especes de pauot" are kinds of poppies; "d'huppe" is apparently some crested plant.[11]

De Nynauld's recipes are the fullest we have. But Summers goes on to quote Weyer, de Lancre, Bodin, Girolamo Cardano, and other classic texts. Robbins has brief but excellent entries on both flying and killing ointments in his *Encyclopedia* (pp. 364-68); and most of the old authors may be consulted in the generous abstracts given by Lea.

What evidence have we that these authorities were not misled by their zeal into recording extravagant fables about witches' ointments, as indeed they were concerning so many of the other aspects of their subject? We have no ironclad evidence, of course; no pot of seventeenth-century ointment has survived. But it is worth noting that two of the best—perhaps the two best—of the old authorities on ointments were decided skeptics. Weyer we know; as for de Nynauld, probably the best source of our knowledge in this area, he was a physician and an antagonist of Bodin's. In his opinion most of the wonders ascribed to the Devil could be explained by simple rational means, namely, the curious poisons which the witches systematically introduced into their systems. Without them, the Devil "cannot even make a fly." "Here," says Summers in horror, "he plainly shows the cloven hoof, and we can only remark that it is surprising such a passage should have been permitted by the censors." Nynauld's arguments he sums up as "flat heresy."[12]

The next question is, what do we know of the way these poisons act on the human body? Answer, a great deal more than we used to, thanks to the tremendous interest in drugs of all kinds in the last couple of decades. The key inquiry was perhaps George Conklin's: "Alkaloids and the Witches' Sabbat," published in 1958.[13] For the first time a true witchcraft scholar took the trouble to gather the new drug information and apply it to the phenomena of the sabbat.

Conklin, who was knowledgeable in many recherché areas, spelled out the implications clearly. One of his technical footnotes is worth reprinting in full.

> The "flying ointment," deriving ultimately no doubt from ancient ceremonial uses of oil, while frequently containing such dramatic elements as baby's fat and such mundane ingredients as soot and parsley, certainly involved monkshood, deadly nightshade, and henbane. Some authorities include Jimson weed. The three major alkaloids definitely used in these ointments then are: aconitine ($C_{34} H_{47} NO_{11}$) from *aconitum napellus* (monkshood); atrophine ($C_{17} H_{23} NO_3$)

from *atropa belladonna* (deadly nightshade); and hyoscyamine $(C_{17} H_{23} NO_3)$ from *hyoscyamus niger* (henbane). If Jimson weed (Datura Stramonium) is included we may add scopolomine $(C_{17} H_{21} NO_4)$. Any question of the toxicological effect of these ingredients used as a salve (as against the indubitable results taken internally) must take into consideration that the ointment was mostly applied to the legs and the vaginal membranes which could convey the toxins to the blood system. Further it should be borne in mind that the louse-bitten skin of a witch was unlikely to be unbroken. Gonzales, Vance, Helpern and Umberger in *Legal Medicine, Pathology and Toxicology*, N.Y.; 1954 (2nd ed.) p. 852, report poisoning from the application of belladonna plaster to the skin. Glaister *(Medical Jurisprudence and Toxicology*, Edinburgh, 1953 (9th ed.), p. 650), states more generally that the use of belladonna as an external application in the form of linament and plaster and as an enema has caused serious and even fatal results. He reports toxic symptoms after the use of a two-grain pessary.[4]

In another footnote (n. 13), Conklin quotes the German toxicologist Gustav Schenk on the effects of belladonna poisoning:

"At the climax of this mood of exhilaration, his excitement grows more intense. *He is no longer master of his senses, which deceive him. He sees nonexistent figures and movements which no one makes. He hears music and sounds when there is complete silence all around him.* The colors of objects before his eyes change: green becomes black and a black surface appears to him a dazzling light. *His confusion grows greater and greater and in this phase he may easily be subordinated to another's will, for he is completely open to influence and will do whatever he is told.*" (My italics.) If Schenk is right, it is indeed a temptation to explain accordingly the docile behavior of initiates at Sabbat ceremonies as well as the power of the cult leader to create such impressions as the real presence of Satan.[15]

Conklin also cites Clark's suppositions that the use of aconite would cause irregular heartbeat, which might, combined with the other effects, give a sense of flight. "It is a little ironical," he concludes, "to find the clinic of the twentieth century giving some credence to the impossible confessions of the sixteenth."[16]

Since 1958, the clinic has accomplished much more. But before considering recent studies, we ought to remind ourselves if only briefly of the enormous world literature of drug-induced hallucination, much of it originating from the great Romantics of the nineteenth century. Ought we to wonder, for example, at the witches' experiences when we remember De Quincey, watching from his bed "vast processions [passing] along in mournful pomp," believing himself "stared at, hooted at, grinned at, chattered at, by monkeys, by paroquets, by cockatoos," or "kissed, with cancerous kisses, by crocodiles?"[17] Baudelaire's hashish-intoxicated hero experienced "the supreme thought"—"I have become God,"[18] while Theophile Gautier, under the influence of the same drug, experienced "monstrosities" and "invisible powers."[19] These experiences did not much differ from those described by Robert Graves in his essay "The Poet's Paradise."[20] There among other things Graves tells of the visions he experienced after eating *psilocybe*, the sacred mushroom of the Aztecs. He had been warned that "whoever nurses evil in his heart sees hideous demons and nameless horrors," and in fact he did at one point perceive a legion of grimacing faces peering at him, but was able to dismiss them with a wave of his hand.[21]

With the mention of the drugs of the New World we enter the latest stage of inquiry into the witch potions. Following the lead of Margaret Murray, a number of young researchers, most of them anthropologists, have continued to explore the possibility of the existence of a genuine witch cult in Europe, having gained new insights and impetus from their studies of drug-oriented sorcerers in South and Central America.

That the Latin-American *bruja* or *brujo*—witch—trafficks widely in drugs has long been known, as has the fact that the primitive tribes of the interior depend upon hallucinogenic agents for many of their rites and ceremonies. Explorers such as Bertrand Flournoy, who in 1953 published an account of his travels among the Jivaro, have remarked on the tremendous prestige of the jungle sorcerers;

"the only organized force and the only authoritative voice which the Jivaro Indian obeys is the power of the witch doctor."[22] Flournoy tells of the powerful alkaloids with which these men drench their systems, *natema,* and the related *ayaguasa,* and *maykua.* Their consciousnesses sensitized and as we might say, liberated, by these drugs, the witch doctors undertake the tribe's healing, its prophecy, and usually, "the responsibility for the murders and warlike excursions that decimate these tribes"[23]—because sickness and misfortune in the Amazon jungles, as in sixteenth-century Europe, are attributed to the hostile wishes of enemies, usually the witch doctors of rival tribes. The witch doctor's devotion to these enormous responsibilities evokes Flournoy's frank admiration: "Next day I looked at Maceo's ravaged face, his glittering eyes which shunned the daylight,[24] and was deeply moved. And yet this exhausted man had been accustomed to alkaloids and stupefacients ever since the day, when, to celebrate his puberty, he had drunk whole jars of hot *natema"* (p. 120).

Flournoy himself tried *natema,* which treated him to horrible visions: "enormous dogs' heads, Indians armed with spears lying in wait for me in the forest, gigantic spiders." He ended by getting very sick to his stomach; but the Indians were sympathetic: "They had been through these torments themselves at their first attempt."[25]

The naturalist Peter Matthiessen is also familiar with the Amazon and its drugs; the plot of his excellent novel *At Play in the Fields of the Lord* (1965) makes use of the alkaloid which he renders *ayahuasca.* His hero, Lewis Moon, having taken an overdose (which, forcing his mind back into the past, provides the machinery of the exposition), finds that in his delirium he recalls patches of technical information:

> The extract of *B. Caapi* is a powerful narcotic and hallucinogen containing phenol alkaloids related to those found in lysergic acid, and whether or not it finds a respectable place in the pharmaceutica of man, it has held for unknown centuries an important place in the culture of Indian tribes of the Amazon basin.

. . . .

B. Caapi,[26] which is named for the *Caapi* of certain
Brazilian Indians, is also the *Camorampi* of the Campa, the
Natema of the Jivaro, the *Ayahuasca* or *haya-huasca* of the
Quechua-speaking peoples, the *Yage* of Equador, the *Soga
de Muerte* of most Spanish South Americans, names
variously translated as "vine of the Devil," "vine of the
Soul," "vine of Death": the Spanish term literally means
"vine-rope of death," the *Soga* referring to the jungle lianas
used commonly as canoe lines, lashings, ropes, etc. In
addition to certain medical properties, the vine can induce
visions, telepathic states, metaphysical contemplation and
transmigration: these conditions are used by the Indians for
the reception of warnings, prophecies and good counsel.
Among many tribes one purpose of the dream state is
identification of an unknown enemy, and the use of it is
thus related to the Jivaro practice of taking *Tsantsa*, or
shrunken heads.[27]

An anthropologist deeply learned in these matters, and at the
same time well-read in the annals of European witchcraft, is
Michael Harner. His work among the Jivaro has convinced him of
the reality of a European witch cult centered on the use of
hallucinogenic drugs. In an important article in *Natural History*
(June-July 1968), Professor Harner makes among others the
following points: that witchcraft should be defined in its widest
sense (one rejected by the skeptics) as acts, both maleficent and
beneficial, carried out by "paranormal" means—that is, spiritual,
nonmaterial agencies; and that in the cases which he documents,
autosuggestion (a favorite explanation of the psychologists) is
impossible, since the witch doctors do their best to *keep* their
intended victims from knowing what is in store for them. Harner
also notes the close resemblance of the visions experienced by the
New World witches—and by himself, when he took the drug—to
those reported by Old World members of the cult: "devilish"
visitations, "bird headed people"[28] and "dragon-like creatures."[29]

The most dramatic revelations of all on this subject, however, for
most people, are those of Carlos Castaneda, a young graduate

student in anthropology at University of California at Los Angeles. It is as if a sixteenth-century witchcraft novice were to turn up suddenly in our midst, alive, bearing proofs, and eager to share them. Castaneda allegedly apprenticed himself to a powerful Mexican *brujo*, a Yaqui Indian known as Don Juan. For the better part of five years he studied the way of becoming a Man of Knowledge; and his studies included careful indoctrination in peyote, jimson weed *(datura)* and hallucinogenic mushrooms (which he thinks may have been *psilocybe*). The phenomena which these drugs and other disciplines produced bear startling resemblances to those reported by Renaissance European witch-hunters, and by European witches themselves.

The book in which Castaneda records all this, *The Teachings of Don Juan: A Yaqui Way of Knowledge*,[30] is fascinating; let me cite here two episodes which deal with two of the principal areas covered in studies of classical European witchcraft: transvection and transformation.

The striking thing is that Don Juan, like the midnight hags of Old World folklore, teaches that the power to fly is attainable to men, with the aid of a certain unguent. His methods of applying it, too, are familiar: the candidate strips himself naked and anoints part of his body with the thick paste—both legs and the feet and especially the genitals. This paste, which Castaneda assisted in preparing, consists principally of pulverized *datura*, with the weevils which infect it, and lard. Castaneda also, and this is significant, was given a stiff *drink*, of extract of *datura* root. The results were as follows:

> Don Juan kept staring at me. I took a step toward him. My legs were rubbery and long, extremely long. I took another step. My knee joints felt springy, like a vault pole; they shook and vibrated and contracted elastically. I moved forward. The motion of my body was slow and shaky; it was more like a tremor forward and up. I looked down and saw Don Juan sitting below me, way below me. The momentum carried me forward one more step, which was even more elastic and longer than the preceding one. And from there I soared. I remember coming down once; then I pushed up

with both feet, sprang backward, and glided on my back. I saw the dark sky above me, and the clouds going by me. I jerked my body so I could look down. I saw the dark mass of the mountains. My speed was extraordinary. My arms were fixed, folded against my sides. My head was the directional unit. If I kept it bent backward I made vertical circles. I changed directions by turning my head to the side. I enjoyed such freedom and swiftness as I had never known before. The marvelous darkness gave me a feeling of sadness, of longing, perhaps. It was as if I had found a place where I belonged—the darkness of the night. I tried to look around, but all that I sensed was that the night was serene, and yet it held so much power. (Pp. 127-28)

Castaneda eventually returned to earth, and found himself naked and sick with a bursting headache, out in the open about a half mile from his master's home, his starting point. But the night-flights of the witches were no longer a matter of pure speculation to him. One point needs reemphasis: "the unguent by itself is not enough," the *brujo* says (p. 129). "The second portion of the weed"—that which Castaneda drank—"is used to fly." It would seem worthwhile to reexamine the European accounts in light of this advice.

Another startling section of the book relates how Don Juan taught his pupil to change himself into an animal, in this case, a crow. Under the influence of a powerful drug, apparently *psilocybe* or some related agent, Castaneda

had the perception of growing bird's legs, which were weak and wobbly at first. I felt a tail coming out of the back of my neck and wings out of my cheekbones. The wings were folded deeply. I felt them coming out by degrees. The process was hard but not painful. Then I winked my head down to the size of a crow. But the most astonishing effect was accomplished with my eyes. My bird's sight!

Later his mentor "tossed him up" and he flew, joining other birds at one point. But his memories of the event were garbled and unhelpful.

After the great success of *The Teachings of Don Juan*, Castaneda brought out several more volumes, which amplify and extend his original findings: *A Separate Reality* (1971), *Journey to Ixtlan* (1972), *Tales of Power* (1974), and *The Second Ring of Power* (1977). Though they established their author as something of a cult figure in his own right, they also brought down upon him the inquiries of an increasingly suspicious group of scholars. These inquiries may be said to have culminated in an exposé by Richard De Mille, *Castaneda's Journey / The Power and the Allegory* (Santa Barbara: Capra Press, 1976). Here De Mille convincingly, though amiably, explodes Castaneda's claims, while identifying the sorcerer's apprentice himself as a multiple-background, multiple-personality figure of the species well known to the bunco squad. De Mille is able to show that Castaneda's accounts of himself and his background are contradictory and confused; his very name is suspect. All Castaneda's findings, too, it seems, were available to him in previously published material, particularly that of Gordon Wasson *(Soma, Divine Mushroom of Immortality* [New York: Harcourt, Brace and World, 1968]). "Don Juan" begins to prove an elusive figure; but not so elusive as his alleged disciple, nor so colorful.

Castaneda's revelations then, disappointingly, may not be accepted as the results of actual research. But as fictions, his works are still worthy of study, although many readers have noted a marked decline in quality after the first volume. We still await proof of the place of hallucinogens in the witchcraft delusion; but at least the time is past when a scholar could say, "it is not an easy matter to decide what the effect of these concoctions may have been!"

9. Salem

 The most famous American venture into the field of witch-hunting took place in Salem, Massachussetts, in 1692. To this day most Americans think that Salem and the Puritans who lived there in the seventeenth century were uniquely wicked or deluded; that Salem was one of the great world centers of the witch persecution. In fact it was no such thing. It was a small and rather insignificant late outburst of a European social phenomenon which had just about run its course. But it was America's biggest witch scandal and we have always been proud of it. Instead we should probably congratulate ourselves on the considerable extent to which we avoided the witch hysteria that tore whole sections of Europe to pieces for several hundred years.

Nevertheless we need a short chapter here to sort out a few facts, because for Americans the Salem trials do have a significance out of all proportion to their place in the world-witchcraft picture. Specifically the student should ask why the hysteria came where and when it did, and who was principally responsible for it. This last is just now being sharply debated. Another important question is this: are the skeptics, who have always dominated discussions of Salem, correct in assuming that the outbreak was pure petty malice fanned to community hysteria; or was there a coven actually in operation in Massachusetts? Did persons there actually "practice witchcraft," along the classic lines laid down by Bodin and Del Rio? Or was it all small-town backbiting and politics?

First of all, the Puritans were no more prone to witch-hunts than anyone else. Surely this should be clear at least to readers of this book, who have watched Catholics and Protestants in Germany, say, vie with one another in persecutory zeal. The Puritans feared and hated witchcraft because they were men of their time, not because they were Puritans. A little reflection will find the origin of this error in American parochialism: in our country the most celebrated witch-hunt was carried out by Puritans; therefore Puritans are the most celebrated witch-hunters. George Lyman Kittredge long ago demolished this notion, anyway, with enormous machinery of logic and evidence, and the student cannot do better than consult him on it.[1]

Secondly, there were no burnings in New England or anywhere else in British America, for the good reason that the English law did not prescribe burning as a punishment for witchcraft. Burning was reserved in England for treason, both high, as rebellion against one's king, or low, as the murder of one's husband. To be sure, witchcraft sometimes figured in these crimes, so that if a witch were convicted of having used her arts to commit treason, she could be burned. But witchcraft per se was a hanging offense, when indeed it was punished by death, which was not always the case by any means.

The cause of the Salem witch troubles was the same as the German, French, or Italian witch troubles, or indeed, any other known. Fundamentally it was this: seventeenth-century European man, like the twentieth-century Jivaro, was in general not capable of conceiving of fortuitious mischance. Epidemics, household accidents, bad luck, drowning, obstruction in one's career—indeed, all irritations whatsoever—were seen as the result of opposing influence, the malign wishes of a neighbor or some other enemy, aided more often than not by professional evildoers: witches, sorcerers, witch doctors. Now Salem, like the rest of New England, had always been precariously fixed: a tiny outpost on the edge of a continent truly dark and inhabited by legions of savages who even at their more quiescent moments were understood to be servants of Satan. The quality of life was, even beyond this paranoid circumstance, particularly hard and trying; that is, disregarding the unknown possibilities of the hinterland, the colonies were engaged in a day-to-day struggle against cold, hunger, and general deprivation which has become proverbial. True, they had for the most part gained a fairly solid footing by the end of the seventeenth century, but even so the year 1692 found Salem unusually hard-pressed.

The Indians were on the warpath, the French were hostile, there were pirates on the seas. The colonists' own English government was not much more pleasant to deal with: not content with imposing crushing taxes, it was in the process of questioning Salem's very constitution. Moreover the winter was exceptionally hard, and there was a smallpox epidemic. So in addition to hardship and danger we may cite *uncertainty*, perhaps the greatest cause of all of community hysteria; the reader will recall the witch outbursts at their height in England during the confused early period of the civil war, and in Germany during the religious broils of the Thirty Years' War.[2]

The origin of the Salem incident was in the harmless custom of a group of girls, or young women, of coming over to the Reverend Samuel Parris's house to listen to his slave Tituba's ghost stories. Tituba was apparently a Carib Indian, not a Negro, as is often stated (as in Robbins's *Encyclopedia*, p. 432).

Her tales were so inspiring that before long they had some of the girls in convulsions: Parris broke up the group but the fits continued. At first these attacks manifested themselves in relatively harmless flouting of authority: the girls had the pleasure of disrupting prayers, throwing Bibles about, and sassing their elders.[3] Events took an ugly turn however, as the hysteria spread to older girls: at the height of the Salem persecutions, the chief accusers were not children, but mostly girls in their late teens.

As people began to become concerned about the girls' behavior and to try to cure them, they naturally began to think of witchcraft as the cause of such preposterous and unheard-of behavior. The girls seem to have taken their cue from the questions of their better-informed elders, and begun to show significant symptoms: not only a (to our minds) very natural distaste for the long Puritan prayers, but a real inability to say them, or the name of God; and they now had visions of the Devil and his ministers, lurking nearby. And they began to name names.

Parris was horrified to learn that one of the women in his congregation had resorted to black magic to fight black magic: she had ordered prepared (by Tituba and her husband, John Indian) a "witch-cake"—a cake made of meal mixed with the afflicted girls' urine which, when fed to the family dog, was supposed to release the sufferers from the spell upon them, or at least allow them to name their tormentors. This it did—"another instance of the efficacy of magic in a society which believes in it," as Chadwick Hansen observes.⁴

The "tormentors" named were "the obvious scapegoats of the community, the vulnerable and weak"⁵—Tituba, who was of course a slave; Sarah Good, a beggar; and Sarah Osborne, who was crippled and moreover, like Good, had a bad reputation in general. They were examined before Judges Hathorne and Corwin, and their depositions implicated others, who were in their turn examined, and identified by the girls as their tormentors, even in court, by spectral means. And so *their* depositions implicated still others, among them now persons of hitherto unimpeached respectability; and the devil was indeed let loose in Massachusetts.

A special court was instituted to try the accused. This was not, to cite yet another controversial point, a trick by the Establishment to railroad the "witches," but rather a signal act of mercy. The judicial proceedings of the colony were at this time in the process of complete revision; if a special court had not been instituted, the accused, innocent and guilty alike (as our ancestors must have supposed them), would have had to languish in jail over many months, perhaps even years, which would have been a severe affliction not only physical but financial, since in those days prisoners were chargeable for their prison expenses.

It is not within the scope of this brief study to give a complete account of the trials. They are fascinating and horrifying examples of human complexity, containing as they do the clear duplicity of some of the girl witnesses, the undoubted hysteric affliction of others, and the truly devious and suspicious behavior of some of the accused (such as would surely provoke present-day magistrates) and the saintly patience of others. An imaginative approach to the actual emotional climate of the events is available in Arthur Miller's play *The Crucible;* among the best of the earlier studies we have Marion Starkey's *The Devil in Massachusetts* (New York, 1949), and *Witchcraft in Old and New England* (1929; reprinted New York, 1958), by Kittredge, who despite his capacious title does not really focus on Salem. We have the classic text, Charles Wentworth Upham's *Salem Witchcraft* (1867), and a number of new studies, some points of which I intend to take up shortly; and best of all,

Cotton Mather's own selection of trial transcripts, gathered together in 1692 with much other matter under the title *The Wonders of the Invisible World* (Boston and London, 1693), and often excerpted and reprinted, as in The Library of Old Authors (London, 1862).

What I should like to do in this chapter is to take up several aspects of the trials, cases of two or three individuals, perhaps, who throw into sharp focus the problems the student must keep in mind as he attempts to come to grips with this material. The first and perhaps the critical problem is simply this: what was actually going on in Salem? Were these really persons there who practiced black magic?

Since 1696, when judge and jury confessed their errors, the opinion has been overwhelming, almost unanimous, that the people of Salem were the victims of hysteria. So they said themselves, in 1696: that they were "sadly deluded and mistaken."[6] Quite recently certain scholars have suggested that all was not delusion: that there actually was witchcraft practiced at Salem. This is one of the contentions of Chadwick Hansen's *Witchcraft at Salem* (New York, 1969), one of the more serious studies published on the subject in recent years.

Many of Hansen's points are well taken: for one, that modern historians, in making merry over the credulity of our ancestors, have only exposed their ignorance of seventeenth-century thought and custom. Hansen is also useful in reminding us of the formidable reality of the afflictions suffered by some of the accusers, who are almost always dismissed as palpable liars, even murderers. Of course, some of them were. And yet the hysteric symptoms which some of them suffered were real. Furthermore Hansen is perfectly correct, and especially valuable in our present fashionably anti-Establishment mood, in pointing out that the Salem persecutions were not, as is often thought, promoted by venal, power-hungry clergymen or vicious judges. The judges it is true were not enlightened beyond their fellow men, which was unfortunate but not criminal in them; the clergy however actually operated in most cases as a restraint upon the persecution fever. This point is perhaps the most valuable contribution of Hansen's book. Elsewhere, however, his conclusions are open to question.

He states emphatically that black magic was practiced in Salem, and his first example is Bridget Bishop, whom he begins by calling "in all probability a practicing witch" (p. 64), but ends by accusing flatly of having "practiced malefic witchcraft" (p. 72), having in the course of his own argumentation convinced himself. What precisely is the evidence against Bridget Bishop? First, she had a thoroughly bad reputation, and not just in general: her own husband had accused her of witchcraft. Secondly, she was malicious; among other people she included Judge Hathorne in her threats.

"But there was much more against Bridget Bishop than her reputation or her malice," Hansen continues (p. 65). The most damning item against her is the testimony of two men, that in taking down a cellar wall of her former house, they had found "several poppets made up of rags and Hogs' bristles with headless pins in them with the points outward."[7] "To be sure," Hansen admits, "the evidence was circumstantial—nobody had seen Bridget Bishop stick the pins in the dolls or bury them in the walls" (p. 65). But it was much less than that! *There were no dolls in evidence.* Surely, with our enormous experience of stimulated imaginations on this subject, or even out-and-out fraud—which some people doubtlessly would have been happy to practice in such good cause as getting rid of a general troublemaker like Bridget Bishop—we must be particularly cautious with such "evidence." We can bring in plenty more of it; the fact, for example, that another person had ghosts appear before him, which accused "the Spectre of Bishop, crying out, *You Murdered us!*"[8] Some saw ghosts, and others saw dolls. And others saw the accused partaking "of a Diabolical Sacrament" or attacking them in the shape of a black pig out in a field. The fact is, there is no limit to what people will swear to, none. It is dangerous to draw forth for belief one out of a multitude of incredible tales.

Similarly, Hansen cites the testimony of Samuel Shattuck, a dyer, to the effect that Bridget Bishop brought him for dyeing "sundry pieces of lace, some of which were so short that I could not judge them fit for any use" (p. 65). From this circumstance Hansen deduces that Bishop was using such articles of cloth for her dolls. Actually, Shattuck very clearly testified that in his opinion the defendant brought the odd pieces of lace to him merely as a subterfuge, a pretext to get into his house for purposes of mischief, which is of the two surely the simpler explanation.[9]

Hansen's other points, in my opinion, are subject to similar objections. There is no evidence still that witchcraft was actually being practiced in Salem, although obviously everyone thought it was, and that was enough, granted the circumstances. Another of Hansen's arguments which should be considered is his spirited defense of Cotton Mather. Now for years Mather has reigned secure as the villain of the piece; the Victorian introduction to my edition of *Wonders of the Invisible World* (London, 1862), accuses him of obstinacy, "vanity," and "credulity." These are mild terms; he has been called much worse.[10] And correspondingly his opponent, the merchant Robert Calef, has been hailed as an apostle of reason and mercy (as recently as in Robbins's *Encyclopedia*, p. 343). Hansen assaults this traditional evaluation forcibly, and unquestionably he damages Calef's reputation. He is able to show him as a rather slippery opponent on occasion, although I do not think he totally demolishes Calef's objections to Mather's proceedings. Calef seems to have treated the Mathers (Cotton and his father Increase) unfairly in his accusations of impropriety in their dealing with afflicted persons. Nevertheless I continue to think Calef justified in some of his objections. For instance, although Cotton Mather admitted that he had asked a certain afflicted girl, Margaret Rule, who it was that was tormenting her, he insisted he charged her on her life not to reveal any names. Calef answered, "It seems improbable that a question should be put whether she knew [them] (or rather who they were), and at the same time to charge her, and that upon her life, not to tell." This remark reveals to Hansen "studied insolence" and "characteristic evasiveness."[11] I must confess that it seems forthright enough to me.

Hansen is able also to rehabilitate Cotton Mather, but only to a point. He reminds us of Mather's consistent opposition to the admission of spectral evidence—which is certainly very telling in his favor—and of his many cautionary remarks to magistrates and ordinary citizens alike. He recalls Mather's temperance in other witchcraft cases. Yet in spite of all, the old zealot will not totally disappear, the man who stopped the crowd from interfering with the execution of the Reverend George Burroughs, the writer who called my ancestor, Susanna Martin, "one of the most impudent, scurrilous, wicked creatures in the world,"[12] for defending herself with bold resolution.

I confess to a personal bias against the man on behalf of this many times great-grandmother of mine, "a Paula Bunyan among witches," according to Marion Starkey.[13] I was told as a child that she had been hanged because she came into Salem on a rainy day without getting her feet wet. That was the story that had been handed down in the family from generation to generation. And when I first took up Mather, I was electrified to find this item among the testimony against her:

> IX *Sarah Atkinson* testify'd, that *Susanna Martin* came from *Amesbury* to their house at *Newbury*, in an extraordinary season, when it was not fit for any to travel. She came (as she said, unto Atkinson) all that long way on Foot. She brag'd and shew'd how dry she was; nor could it be perceived that so much as the Soles of her Shoes were wet. *Atkinson* was amazed at it; and professed, that she should herself have been wet up to the knees, if she had then came so far; but *Martin* reply'd *she scorn'd to be Drabbled!* It was noted, that this Testimony upon her Trial, cast her in a very singular confusion. (Pp. 145-46)

As well it might. It must be remembered of course that roads in that day were nothing like what they are now, and that Susanna's accomplishment was a most unusual one. But the real lesson of the incident is how fatally any little boast might recoil upon a person, in an atmosphere so charged with fear and hatred. Elsewhere Susanna Martin bore herself bravely:

> MAGISTRATE: How comes your appearance to hurt these?
> [the witnesses]
> MARTIN: How do I know? He that appeared in the Shape of *Samuel*, a glorified Saint, may appear in any ones Shape.
> (Pp. 139-40)

When the judge asked her the meaning of the afflicted persons being flung to the ground at approaching her, she said, "I cannot tell; it may be, the Devil bears me more Malice than another"(p. 140).

Other charges against her were stock: she had bewitched cattle, she (or a demonic servant) had attacked people in the form of a cat, and so on. Mather's account of her, as of the other four defendants whose trials he uses, is openly hostile and abusive. And it is here, upon the jagged rock of *The Wonders of the Invisible World*, that the rehabilitation of Mather founders. Hansen acknowledges the awkwardness of the book: "it is necessary to recall his sanity and temperance now because the book he wrote in October of 1692, *The Wonders of the Invisible World*, was anything but temperate" (pp. 168-69).

Hansen's only excuse for the man is that he felt called upon to vindicate the good name of the magistrates, to defend their good faith, even though he had disapproved of their methods. That is a reason, whether the true one or not we cannot tell; but it is not much of an excuse. Hansen cannot enlist much sympathy for the author of such a work. Mather was no villain but on the contrary an able and conscientious man of his own time. He was far from being the best of those in Salem in 1692, however; and he stubbornly abstained from any suggestion that he had at any time throughout the trials been wrong in his words or deeds, even after many of the other participants had confessed their errors.

For that was the startling thing which eventually grew out of the Salem trials. Twenty people suffered death, and two were "known to have died in jail," as Kittredge puts it:[14] a terrible toll, no matter if slight compared to the hundreds of thousands slaughtered in Europe. Salem got the poison out of its system within one year—a deliverance unknown anywhere else—and then, after a few months more of self-study, decided that it had been terribly wrong, proceeded to confess its guilt openly to the world, and never afterward reverted to the witch mania. As Kittredge says: "The most remarkable things about the New England prosecution were the rapid return of the community to its habitually sensible frame of mind and the frank public confession of error made by many of those who had been implicated" (p. 365).

The nature of this error has been much clarified in some recent studies by Paul Boyer and Stephen Nissenbaum.[15] In their book

Salem Possessed, they reveal the events of 1692 as the mere tip of the iceberg, the culmination of nearly thirty years of community conflict. "Salem," where the persecutions occurred, was Salem *Village* (now Danvers), a conservative backwater full of dissatisfaction and mostly inarticulate, or at least ineffective, rage against Salem *Town*, the modern-day Salem, already in the late seventeenth century a boomtown which had indeed made a pact with the devil, if the devil be considered "wealth, sensual pleasures, and worldly sophistication."[16] Because Salem Village was not a legally constituted body, but technically still a part of the hated and feared Salem Town, it was denied the ordinary measures of civic reform; in fact, it experienced the greatest possible difficulties in establishing and maintaining even a church of its own.

These deep, basic social and political dissensions were aggravated, Boyer and Nissenbaum show, by personal quarrels, especially those between the Putnams, a powerful old family on the decline, and the Porters, representatives of the new wealth and the new worldliness. As the student will recognize at once, it was the failing Putnam family which gave key support to the witchcraft persecutions. Putnam frustration reached its peak when a Putnam stepmother maneuvered her own son Joseph into the family inheritance, cutting out the older children of the first marriage. This Joseph Putnam then crowned the betrayal by joining with the Putnam's rivals, the progressive Porter clan.

With considerable ingenuity Boyer and Nissenbaum trace the relationships among the accused witches, scapegoats indeed for the most part, "outsiders," "mobile," and "lacking in deference."[17] (Surely the last qualification fits Goody Martin.) These were the available victims; progress itself, which the villagers both feared and yet in some sort desired, lay beyond their reach. Even the hated Putnam stepmother, Mary Keren Putnam, was too highly placed to abide their anger, which then, according to Boyer and Nissenbaum, was sublimated into the witch-hunting.

> By first projecting upon others the unacknowledged
> impulses which lay within themselves, and then absolving
> those they had accused, the accusers could bring such

impulses into the open, gain at least temporary mastery over them, and thereby confirm their commitment to social values in which they very much wanted to believe. It is surely no coincidence that not one of the confessing witches was hanged.[18]

This judgment seems persuasive, and it is supported by many other findings, including a brilliant study of the four ministers who served Salem Village between 1672 and 1692. The most important of these of course is Samuel Parris, whom Boyer and Nissenbaum characterize as a loser, a failed businessman with a distinct touch of paranoia about him; a niggler who insisted on numerous petty concessions in his dealings with others, which he then failed to get into print. It is worth noticing that his successor, Joseph Green, a man of much different personality, was able to reconcile the struggling factions and bring peace to the exhausted combatants, thus setting the stage for the public recantation and confession of 1696.

Something good, something for Americans to be proud of, certainly did happen in Salem then; not the lurid details of the greatest witch-hunt in the world, but the rare, almost unheard-of spectacle of a community's admitting to its bigotry and hate and injustice, and vowing to repeat them no more.

10.Occultists and Transcendentalists: Witchcraft Today

"Witches feel they owe a debt to Dr. Murray for being the first to tell them that they were not the poisoners, diabolists or imposters that practically all other writers call them." So wrote witchcraft cult leader Gerald B. Gardner, in 1954.[1] Other observers believe that the booming contemporary witchcraft cult owes Margaret Murray not only for its reputation, but for its very existence.

One of these was the late Julian Franklyn, author of several books on the occult, controversialist and a stern monitor of the large British witchcraft establishment.

> This Gerald Gardner [he writes], who spent many years in an official post in Malaya, could not fail to observe native witchcraft, but there is no reason to suppose that he had, at that period, discovered that he was himself a witch. The discovery does not seem to ante-date his reading of the works on the subject from Margaret Murray's pen. Having made a collection of weapons and native odds and ends he set up, in 1950, his witchcraft museum in the Isle of Man.
>
> Opinions concerning Gardner are mixed. He is the author of two books, *Witchcraft Today* (1954) and *The Meaning of Witchcraft* (1959). Both of these works are, apparently, directed to a 'popular' readership. It is certain that neither of them reveals scholarship, nor esoteric knowledge. He was personally abnormal: a flagellant and an exhibitionist: he

also painted very bad pictures of voluptuous witches being burned to death. His flair for self-advertisement enabled him to attract attention to himself, and to gather together numerous social and sexual misfits who organized themselves into covens of thirteens and pretended to be witches. A few of them had read a little in the realm of black magic and other occult practices, others of them were herbalists and astrologers; there were to be found in their ranks hysterics, and folk with semi-developed mediumistic powers. Exhibitionists and nudists, they were not witches. They considered themselves rather superior to ordinary folk: they were far too enlightened to believe in the devil; they were the remnants of that pre-Christian European paganism of which they had never heard before Margaret Murray's work brought it to their notice.

The only harm these people ever did, according to Franklyn, "was to provide an organization (for want of a better word) to which the really evil diabolists could attach themselves."[2]

If I quote Franklyn at length, it is because his remarks provide a useful summary of the attitude of scholarship in general toward the witchcraft position which I have identified as "transcendentalist." Before giving Gardner a chance to speak on his own behalf, let us take a moment to reflect on some historical precedents of the practical application of occult studies.

There have always existed, as far as I can determine, individuals and groups devoted to the cultivation of "supernatural powers," that is, powers inexplicable by or hostile to current religious and scientific systems. Some of these individuals and groups are messianic or apocalyptic, as in the case of the Mormons, Rogerenes, Dorrellites, or the Live for Evers, of Sutton, Massachusetts. Others are purely fraudulent. Casanova was one who turned a little occult knowledge, an engaging person, and a lively patter into gold. At one point in his spectacular career he was called upon to cast a horoscope. Never mind that he had never done so before:

. . . my predictions concerning the future raised no doubt. I risked nothing, for they were all buttressed with "ifs."

The "ifs" always constituted the whole science of astrologers, who have all been fools or knaves. Reading over the horoscope and finding it brilliant, I was not surprised. Being an accomplished cabalist, I must also be an accomplished astrologer.[3]

Casanova was a pleasant enough rogue, who was at least honest with himself some of the time; the difficult cases are those of people who are part messiah, part confidence man. Many of the most celebrated practitioners of the doubtful sciences seem to have been just such people; certainly the most famous among modern occultists was.

This is the gentleman whom Julian Franklyn was about to cite, when we cut him off, as a dangerous diabolist, the leader of a "devil-worshipping dark brotherhood of malefic, anti-human beasts": Aleister Crowley. Franklyn echoes the newspapers of Crowley's day in calling the magician a "drug addict and sexual pervert of the most revolting kind,"[4] but the student who looks impartially into Crowley's enormous *oeuvre* may gain a different impression.

The best way to start is with Crowley's *apologia*, his *Confessions*, recently reissued in a fine new edition by Hill and Wang.[5] This enormous volume (960 pages) reveals the man in his full complexity. To quote from my own review of it,

> Crowley was a world celebrity through the twenties and thirties, a poet (and in his own estimation a great one), painter, traveler, chess player and first-rate mountaineer as well as a master of magic, narcotics and sex. "He wore a special Perfume of Immortality," Richard Cavendish reports, "made of one part ambergris, two parts musk and three parts civet, which gave him a peculiar odor, but which he said attracted women and also horses, which always whinnied after him in the streets." He makes a brief but brilliant appearance in Hemingway's *A Moveable Feast*. Despite his perfume of Immortality, he died in 1947 at 72, having gone through a fortune as well as a sturdy constitution.[6]

Crowley's interest in the occult was almost certainly fostered by his unwilling membership, as a child, in the Plymouth Brethren, that particularly repressed and repressive sect of English fundamentalists made notorious by Sir Edmund Gosse in *Father and Son*. The first, and best, part of the *Confessions* consists of a brilliant dissection of late Victorian manners and morals, somewhat in the manner of Shaw; later on there are excellent accounts of Crowley's travels on foot through places as diverse as China, Mexico, Tibet, and Spain. When he gets on his "magickal"[7] horse, Crowley becomes tiresome; and when he insists on his poetry he turns pallid; everywhere else he is amusing and entertaining. "Darjeeling," he says, is "the last hope of the unmarriageable shabby-genteel," and "lousy with young ladies whose only idea of getting a husband is to practice the piano."[8]

We are delighted with his triumphs over his own ugly, pious family, as when he encountered an uncle who had written an opus called *The Two Wicked Kings*, which dealt with two great tyrants who oppressed young men. These, it turned out were Smo-King and Drin-King. "'But, my dear uncle,'" Crowley said, "'you have forgotten to mention a third, the most dangerous and deadly of all.' He couldn't think who that was. I told him."[9]

Crowley can also poke fun at himself, as when he catches himself crowing over the rise in value of one of his books: "I refuse to feel any satisfaction at knowing that, published at ten shillings, it is now quoted at three pounds, fifteen shillings at a minimum. (Then why mention it? Oh, shut up.)" (P. 504.) William Seabrook, who knew Crowley well, sums him up thus: "I am possibly too casual, but feel that the British in general . . . have been a bit heavy in their attitude toward the Master Therion [a cult name of Crowley's]. If he had been an American, I can't help feeling that we'd have had more fun with him."[10]

Aleister Crowley exemplifies a central problem facing the student trying to come to grips with twentieth-century witchcraft: to what extent are occultists like him to be included in witchcraft studies? Are Diabolists, Satanists, to be reckoned as witches? (To what extent Crowley was a diabolist is questionable, in spite of the press and Franklyn.) First of all, it will have to be granted that there is a certain amount of diabolist activity today, especially in England

and California, whence we hear of all sorts of outrages—desecration, sacrilege, vandalism, even murder. It is known, for example, that Charles Manson, while not nominally a Satanist, was in touch with Satanist groups and had absorbed some of their philosophy.[11] Among recent sensational British cases are the Meon Hill murder, near Lower Quinton, Warwickshire, 1945; the Bramber, Sussex case, in 1963; the Tottenham Park Cemetery desecrations of Hallowe'en, 1968; and the Tunbridge Wells desecration early in 1969. In California we have the Church of Satan in the United States, a properly incorporated religion claiming nine thousand members worldwide. Its leader is the celebrated Anton La Vey, who among his other credits numbers the role of the Devil in the film *Rosemary's Baby*.

But are the perpetrators of these crimes and roles to be called witches? Apparently not. In our time a gulf has opened between the witch and her alleged former master. In the sixteenth century, anyone devoted to Satan was a witch; that was what one called a devil-worshiper, by definition. The vigorous renunciation of the devil and all his works by contemporary witchcraft is a curious but well-documented phenomenon, and a strong indication that the skeptics are right in ascribing the new cult to the impetus of Margaret Murray.

Leaving the occultists, then (although with some reluctance) as no longer centrally involved in witchcraft,[12] we turn to the last portion of our study, investigation of the new witchcraft cult proper. It will soon become evident that this path is not an easy one, either. As Raymond Lamont Brown remarks, "two characteristics seem to identify modern British witches: their love of ceremony and their inherent schismatic tendencies."[13] Both points hold true for witches in America and elsewhere. There seem to be hundreds of contending cults, most of which sooner or later make their professions in print, under such titles as "The Real Witchcraft," "The Truth About Witchcraft," and "Witchcraft From the Inside." To investigate all, or even most of these effusions, would be tedious and unrewarding; but in the hope of getting some idea of contemporary "witchcraft," however worthy it may be of the name, we ought to consult two or three.

Certainly we should take a closer look at Gerald Brosseau

Gardner, whom we left in the crushing embrace of Julian Franklyn, who, if he was demonstrably too hard on Crowley, may be suspected of having been too severe with Gardner as well. A more favorable estimate of the so-called "King of the Witches" is that given by C. H. Wallace in his *Witchcraft in the World Today:*

> He was not a medical doctor, although his knowledge of herbal medicines was extensive. He was a Doctor of Philosophy and a Doctor of Literature, the author of a comprehensive study of witchcraft, one of the world's leading experts in that field and the owner and director of the Museum of Magic and Witchcraft in Castleton, Isle of Man.[14]

Gardner's *Witchcraft Today* (with an introduction by Margaret Murray) is largely refried *Witch-Cult in Western Europe*, sandwiched between an opening chapter in which "the author is permitted to write about witches 'from the inside'" (p. 17), and a lengthy recapitulation in which Gardner records more of his own observations and answers questions about witch practices. The former section treats, with considerable naïveté, of the traditional dislike of witches: "I have attended many of the cult rites, and I declare that most of what he [Pennethorne Hughes] says is simply not true" (p. 22). There are no blasphemies, no inverted crosses, no orgies. Gardner describes how couples "join hands and jump over the blazing cauldron," then dance and feast. "Is there anything very wicked or awful in all this?" (p. 25). We may be sure, he says, that witches pay no homage to the devil (p. 23).

In the last section, Gardner comments upon certain practices traditionally ascribed to witches: among them transformation into animals—"to them it is only a joke" (p. 139); infanticide—"ridiculous" (p. 146); and witch-marks—"the ones I know have never heard of it," except in Murray's books (p. 149). Along the way, he occasionally adds other material out of his own knowledge, often to refute Hughes, whose opinions are anathema. In one passage which has become well known, he tells how British witches cast spells to stop Hitler's projected invasion of England, "just as their great grandfathers had done to Boney and their remoter forefathers had done to the Spanish Armada"[15] (p. 104).

One may avoid judgments as harsh as Franklyn's, and still not place much reliance on Gardner's work, most of which consists of restatements of Margaret Murray's theories, themselves much eroded by recent scholarship; most uncritical acceptance of the claims of the cult; and a rather fanciful approach to facts in general—for example, he speaks of "nine million victims in Europe who went to the stake"[16] on the charge of witchcraft—an absurd overstatement. (An estimate one-tenth as high would be considered excessive by most scholars.)

Another partisan of the modern witchcraft cult is Hans Holzer, the well-known psychic investigator. His book *The Truth About Witchcraft*[17] was brought forward with much din of publicity. Here again we have the standard opening: the "few books" that "deal realistically" with witchcraft "are either antiquated or full of fictional concepts."[18] With special permission, Holzer engages to set the record straight. And certainly he has penetrated to the heart of the contemporary cult; he has eye-witnesses' accounts of initiation ceremonies, rites, celebrations, dress, incantations, and every other detail of witchcraft as it is presently practiced, especially in England and the United States.

We are present at the initiation of Nikki, "about twenty-one," into a London coven. Amid much ceremony the attractive candidate, blindfolded and robed, is brought forward and bound hand and foot. "These measures are purely symbolic," Holzer says, "and do not carry any erotic implications" (p. 18). She is then stripped naked, symbolically scourged and kissed on the feet, knees, sexual organs, breasts and mouth. More ritual follows, including the high priest's eventual stripping himself, after which he performs "the final act of the initiation as he saw it: cunnilingual contact with her sexual organs as a symbol that the ultimate life force to worship is the force of creation" (p. 24). By the end of the ceremony Nikki "seemed excited and almost floating on air" (p. 25); but Holzer warns away the prurient once more: "Again, and all my occasional levity aside, the kiss in witchcraft is not a smooch. It is a truly brotherly expression devoid of all sexual connotations, more like the kiss-on-the-cheek a French general bestows on a hero being given the Legion of Honor" (p. 98).

One of the best features of Holzer's book is his accounts of prominent present-day witches, like Louise Huebner of Los Angeles or thereabouts, who spends most of her psychic energy influencing politicians; or Dr. H. Sloane, the "cardopractor" of Toledo, and a Californian named Ed: "the trouble with Ed is not his belief in witches but his other enterprises, which are not everybody's cup of tea. He is probably a leading, if not the leading, protagonist for nudism in the state of California" (p. 87). I confess myself particularly drawn to the Boston couple, Witch Leslie and her husband, Bishop Alfred L. Qualls, D.D., D.M. And who could forget Holzer's account of his interview with Sybil Leek (whom he has hypnotized):

> ". . . we draw energy from the trees—if you don't have a tree you die. We always succeed because we know the powers."
>
> "Where do these powers come from, apart from living beings and trees?"
>
> "They come from the moon. The trees go up toward the moon. The moon comes down from the sky between the trees and it makes you feel very warm. Moonlight is warm." (P. 133).

One thing may be said of Holzer, he is a professional writer, who is not afraid to entertain his public. His merry excursion through the world of witches is in marked contrast to the stately movements of many of the witches themselves, whose attitude toward their work is characterized by a high seriousness. Larking spirits like the famous Sybil Leek are frowned on by these: in a recent book, Raymond Buckland, a prominent Long Island witch, takes her angrily to task (or seems to—she is identified as "this unknown woman"): "it must be said," he concludes, "that this woman has said so much nonsense about the Craft; has contradicted herself so frequently, that it is amazing she is still taken seriously by anyone."[19]

Indeed, witches, deprived of the unifying force of persecution, are fighting among themselves as never before. Wallace gleefully records the free-for-all for supremacy in England at Gardner's death in 1964; according to him, Gardner left a "large sum of money" as well as a museum and "a squabbling group of follow-ers." [20] Meanwhile there are as many different kinds of witchcraft in this country, apparently, as there are covens. All these groups publish industriously. Among other items of particular interest, I should cite *Real Magic* by twenty-two-year-old Philip Emmons Isaac Bonewits, "the nation's first academically credited magi-cian." His A.B. diploma from the University of California, with a major in magic, is reproduced on the back of his bookjacket. [21]

Another accomplished young sorcerer is Paul Huson, who has followed up his *Mastering Witchcraft*, a complete book of recipes for the aspiring witch, with a weighty new volume on the Tarot. [22] A truly remarkable production is *Servants of the Devil*, a profusely illustrated *children's book* on the subject by Thomas Aylesworth. [23]

The contemporary witchcraft bibliography bids fair to be as weighty as that of past ages. If much of the material is absurd, it may not be the less interesting to our descendants for that. Surely it does not surpass in foolishness the fancies of the sixteenth-century divines, the alarums of the retired jurists of the Renaissance. It seems that we must leave witchcraft as we found it: muddled, smeared with all the confusions of the ages. Witches now deny the devil as heartily as their forebears were supposed to have denied Christ; and in our time it is the anthropologist who flies through the air reeking of poisoned oils.

We shall never know what *really* happened to James H. Neal, the hero of our first chapter, because ultimately it is reality itself that shrinks from our studies. Witchcraft seems to belong to that portion of man's life which is called into being by the oppression of "reality." Therefore we cannot doubt that, whatever new orthodoxies may arise, even that most confining of them all, utter license, there will endure the desperate need for the unknowable, the inexplicable, and the strange. Faced with the issue of such deep urges as these, the scholar must lay by his hopes for Truth Absolute, and console himself with such pleasant by-products as he may obtain, like those granted by the spirit recorded by John Aubrey: "Being demanded, whether a good Spirit, or a bad? returned no answer, but disappeared with a curious Perfume and most melodious Twang." [24]

11. Second Thoughts

After some forty years of turning my mind upon the phenomenon of witchcraft, I am convinced that the skeptics are largely correct, that 95 percent of our data can be explained by human greed, hysteria, paranoia, perversity, and outright fraud. That leaves, however, the perplexing 5 percent. Can greed, or fraud, or even perversity explain the injuries to the hero of our first chapter, the unfortunate Mr. James Neal? Let us consider a bit further the suggestion which I made, that he had unwittingly participated in the psychic life of Ghana.

Examples of this sort of participation—that of "civilized" men and women in primitive, barbaric beliefs or rites—are well known both to history and to imaginative literature; we might term it the "Heart of Darkness" syndrome after its most famous fictional exposition. Is it really possible to "go native" mentally, as well as physically? Judging from the mass of material available, it seems that the answer must be yes.

Let us leave Africa, and turn to the New World and the remarkable case of Mr. David St. Clair. St. Clair, a well-educated, sophisticated American journalist, fell in love with Brazil, and lived there for twelve years. In his book *Drum and Candle* (New York: Doubleday, 1971), he tells how he gradually became accustomed to the pervasive Brazilian spiritism, Umbanda,[1] or as we often call it, "voodoo." With familiarity came, perhaps, acceptance. One day St. Clair found himself hexed.

It began when he announced to his maid that he would be leaving Brazil for a new assignment in Greece. The maid, whom he calls Edna, had gradually become his majordomo and shared in his prosperity and importance; naturally, she was deeply troubled by his proposed departure. From that time nothing went right for him: monies due him miscarried; his personal relationships fell apart; even his health began to fail. Not only could he not go to Greece, he was in danger of utter collapse.

Eventually Brazilian friends told him, "Someone has put the evil eye on you. Your paths have been closed!"

St. Clair rejected utterly the spiritist theories of his misfortunes: "Nonsense! I don't believe in all that! I'm just having a run of bad luck, that's all." But his friends persisted and soon identified Edna as the source of the trouble (so far it sounds remarkably like witchcraft in Salem Village). Still protesting, St. Clair allowed his friends to take him, and Edna, to a Umbanda session to remove the curse. After many curious rites the God-ridden priestess identified Edna, to her face, as the person who had bewitched him. Still St. Clair resisted: "I don't believe it! This woman is my friend!"

But when the priestess (invested with the diabolical god Exú) removed the curse and redirected it with double force at its originator, all St. Clair's luck changed, and misfortune fell upon Edna. "You don't like me," Exú told him, "you think I'm a fraud. You will see. The future will show you that Exú can be your friend."

Three days later, St. Clair's money matters took a sudden turn for the better. The woman who had broken up with him requested a reconciliation. His health recovered and with it, his spirits. But Edna began to fail and finally confessed that she had indeed put the original curse on him, working in the classical way with bits of his clothing—his stockings—and powders for his food. She wept, embraced him, and left forever.

St. Clair sums up: "Do I, a White, educated Christian American believe in the powers of the Brazilian spirits? I cannot truthfully answer no. I must answer, truthfully, that I do."

Climate of belief, if we wish to call it that, is apparently a powerful force, one that shapes our lives as well as those of "primitives" or "superstitious natives." "Not only do we influence our reality," says Gary Zukav, "but, in some degree, we actually create it." Zukav is speaking not of life in Ghana or Brazil, but of the general human condition; we shall hear much more from him presently. But first consider the power of climate of belief in other areas, that of sport, for example. Do our continual advances in track and field show that we are superior to our ancestors? Or do they rather indicate a change in the climate of belief? The first person to run the marathon, Pheidippides, collapsed and died from the effort, although he was a professional runner (he had also, to be fair, fought in the battle of Marathon). Nowadays, little girls and old men run the marathon distance of twenty-two miles without suffering much discomfort. Does this diminish the accomplishment of the Greek hero?

No, because for him there was no path. His feat was a wonder to his contemporaries for that reason; but in our present climate of belief it is possible for almost anyone to run the marathon. Pheidippides is our path. Consider that in our own time Roger Bannister, the first person to run a four-minute mile, collapsed from the effort upon crossing the finish line; he was establishing a path for those who succeeded him, who now run such distances with little difficulty.

One great objection to "climate of belief," as to any other force that purportedly acts on people in such a way as to bypass normal sensual experience—ESP, psychokinesis, intuition—is that it breaks the laws of physics. No matter what Ghanaians think, says the disbeliever smugly, they can't push people off grandstands by invisible agencies, nor can Brazilians ruin you financially by stealing your socks.

The answer seems to be that climate of belief is just another way of describing the activity of the human mind, which increasingly seems capable of performing all these "supernatural" feats all on its own. Yes, Newtonian physics has no place for these phenomena, and discards them abruptly, even angrily.[2] Yet twentieth-century physics has found itself to be increasingly estranged from Newton. The all-encompassing world of subatomic particles, for instance, seems never to have heard of Newton, but it does know Buddha! Thus physicists have been dragged, kicking and screaming, into the realm of metaphysics.

The new theory that so far has withstood every test is quantum mechanics. The way it handles the enormous uncertainties that new discoveries in particle physics, astronomy, and math have brought upon us is to reflect them in its own nature—contrary to classical, or Newtonian, physics, which had the universe running like a clock. But our new techniques have opened vast new realms to us, realms that do not always seem guided by "logic." Rather, as Plato (to say nothing of the Buddhists) maintained, it is our comfortable, logical physical life on earth that is illusion—the closer we get to "reality" (a term itself brought into question by quantum mechanics), the more uncertain things become.

I myself enter this area of thought like a child putting out to sea in a cockleshell, but I have as my guide a most illuminating text, a layman's guide to quantum mechanics called *The Dancing Wu Li Masters*, by Gary Zukav. This highly acclaimed study was recommended to me by my eldest son, to whom it had been assigned as preparatory reading for his advanced physics course. Almost all my remarks about the new physics are drawn from this book, which I have read and reread, I hope with understanding. It must be remembered, however, that physicists themselves are still at odds over many of these new concepts.

It is refreshing to hear a leading contemporary physicist describe physics as, "among other things, an attempt to harmonize with a much greater entity than ourselves, requiring us to seek, formulate and eradicate first one and then another of our most cherished prejudices and oldest habits of thought, in a never-ending quest for the unattainable."[3] That is not the way physics was presented to me in my junior year of high school, in 1947!

Quantum mechanics is closely allied not only to philosophy, but also to theories of perception. One of the first and most disturbing aspects is its uncertainty: what we study seems to take its shape from our studying it. This seeming paradox has been demonstrated repeatedly at the subatomic level, where *"we cannot observe something without changing it."*[4] According to Heisenberg's uncertainty principle, we can never know exactly what we want to know about subatomic particles: if we establish their position, then we cannot establish their momentum, and vice versa. This has been repeatedly demonstrated in experiments. The very light by which we see is inadequate to observe particles; and if we try another method, such as gamma rays, our observation actually knocks what we are observing out of its orbit.

Confounding experiences such as this led to the formation of a new theory that would explain them. One of the key experiments, as I understand it, was that which attempted to identify the nature of light. Light is made up of waves; this can be demonstrated in experiments, and has been since Thomas Young's double-slit experiment in 1803. But it can also be demonstrated that light is made up of particles. Which is it, waves or particles? Both can't be correct, or can they? Zukav calls this "fundamental wave-particle duality" "fundamental to quantum mechanics."[5]

To treat with brutal abruptness a problem that has occupied some of the best minds in the world for years, the answer seems to be that light can be either waves or particles, *depending on how you look at it.* It is our observation of things, physicists began to find to their confusion, that makes them what they are.

Thus physics began in spite of itself, and with great resistance from many physicists, to reopen questions that it had thought settled hundreds of years ago. "The rational part of our psyche, typified by science, began to merge again with that other part of us which we had ignored since the 1700s, our irrational side," says Zukav.[6] "Philosophically," he writes, "the implications of quantum mechanics are psychedelic. Not only do we influence our reality, but, in some degree, we actually *create* it" (emphasis Zukav's).

The implications about what we have hitherto termed, most inaccurately, "the supernatural," are clear. Not that quantum mechanics can prove the reality of ghosts, or ESP, or hexes. Quantum mechanics can't prove anything, it just predicts probabilities. That is one reason it is so difficult to grasp, even for — especially for — classical physicists. Quantum mechanics reflects accurately the new world of uncertainty which our study of subatomic particles, and to a certain extent, astronomy, has revealed.

Among the other studies that found their way into quantum mechanics are Einstein's theories of relativity. Einstein himself resisted quantum theory, yet it can subsume his theories as well as it can Newton's; quantum mechanics does not "invalidate" Newton, of course, it merely subsumes him. According to Einstein's "ultimate vision," Zukav tells us, such concepts as "gravity," "energy," and even "matter" do not exist. They are only "mental creations." Even without Einstein, simple logic leads us down this path: if particles are waves, and vice versa, then matter and energy are one. It is just as the Buddhists have been saying for centuries: all things in the universe are one, all experience and all matter are one, and have always existed. As Zukav sums it up, "There is nothing but space-time and motion and they, in effect, are the same thing. Here is an exquisite presentation, in completely Western terms, of the most fundamental aspect of Taoist and Buddhist philosophies."[7]

Zukav, although he repeatedly makes these comparisons between the new physics and Eastern religions, does not venture far into "the supernatural," although he clearly provides the basis for such an expedition: "The real problem is that we are used to looking at the world simply. We are accustomed to believing that something is there or it is not there. Whether we look at it or not, it is either there or not there. Our experience tells us that the physical world is solid, real, and independent of us. Quantum mechanics says, simply, that this is not so."[8]

Let us now look into some cases of "supernatural" behavior in the light of these findings. Many people know the story of the actor James Dean and his untimely death. In fact, a regular cult has grown up around him, as around other figures like Valentino and Elvis Presley. But how many know that Dean was warned of his impending death, a full week before, under the most unlikely circumstances?

This event, which rose to my mind from an enormous collection of similar stories, is recounted in Alec Guinness's autobiography, *Blessings in Disguise.*

> In the autumn of 1955 I went to Los Angeles to make my first Hollywood film, *The Swan,* with Grace Kelly and Louis Jourdan. I arrived, tired and crumpled, after a sixteen-hour flight from Copenhagen. Thelma Moss, who had written the film script of *Father Brown* (*The Detective* in the USA), had said she wished to take me out to dinner my first night in town. We arrived at three restaurants of repute at each of which we were refused admission because she was wearing slacks (ah, far-off days), and finally settled for a

delightful little Italian bistro, where she was confident of a welcome. When we got there—Los Angeles is an endless city to drive through—there was no table available. As we walked disconsolately away I said, "I don't care where we eat or what. Just something, somewhere." I became aware of running, sneakered feet behind us and turned to face a fair young man in sweat-shirt and blue-jeans. "You want a table?" he asked. "Join me. My name is James Dean." We followed him gratefully, but on the way back to the restaurant he turned into a car-park, saying, "I'd like to show you something." Among the other cars there was what looked like a large, shiny, silver parcel wrapped in cellophane and tied with ribbon. "It's just been delivered," he said, with bursting pride. "I haven't even driven it yet." The sports-car looked sinister to me, although it had a large bunch of red carnations resting on the bonnet. "How fast is it?" I asked. "She'll do a hundred and fifty," he replied. Exhausted, hungry, feeling a little ill-tempered in spite of Dean's kindness, I heard myself saying in a voice I could hardly recognise as my own, "Please, never get in it." I looked at my watch. "It is now ten o'clock, Friday the 23rd of September, 1955. If you get in that car you will be found dead in it by this time next week." He laughed. "Oh, shucks! Don't be so mean!" I apologised for what I had said, explaining it was lack of sleep and food. Thelma Moss and I joined him at his table and he proved an agreeable, generous host, and was very funny about Lee Strasberg, the Actors' Studio and the Method. We parted an hour later, full of smiles. No further reference was made to the wrapped-up car. Thelma was relieved by the outcome of the evening and rather impressed. In my heart I was uneasy— with myself. At four o'clock in the afternoon of the following Friday James Dean was dead, killed while driving the car.[9]

Still we must consider the source. Is Guinness a fanciful man, a quack, a fraud? I think not. The tremendous critical ovation that greeted his book emphasized particularly the author's modesty and candor. Events such as the one quoted play a minuscule part in his story. Let us suppose that he actually did blurt out a warning to James Dean. How could this have been possible?

First, notice that his physical nature was oppressed. In almost every story of this kind, the seer, or protagonist, is in some sort of physical distress, often self-induced, like the mortifications of the flesh practiced by hermits, mystics, and dervishes. It is common for "seers" to have suffered some serious illness before finding their gift. Note that Guinness was exhausted after a long flight. One suggestion is that the mind is thus partially freed from the body's all-consuming embrace—or that, in Freudian terms, the grip of the superego is weakened, as when one experiences intoxication from alcohol, cannabis, or other drugs.

With his mind thus "freed" from interference from the earthbound body, or just its own most logical sequences, is it possible that the seer may get a glimpse of such a universe as quantum mechanics, and Buddhism, describe? A universe in which chronology is a comfortable, necessary illusion? "Few physicists believe in telepathy," Zukav remarks, "but some physicists do believe either that at a deep and fundamental level there is no such thing as 'independent real situations' of things which have interacted in the past but which are spatially separated from each other, or that changing the measuring device in area A *does* change 'the real factual situation' in area B."[10] Or, as some Eastern religions teach, "reality" may be fully stretched before us, both past and future as well as the present, but our necessarily limited point of view precludes our grasping the whole. "We are a three-dimensional people who cannot perceive, but who can deduce that we are living in a four-dimensional universe."[11] Time, of course, is the fourth dimension.

Note how this approach sheds light on otherwise totally incomprehensible (to me) accounts such as that of Agnes Sampson's revelations to King James, in our sixth chapter. True, she was very likely on the verge of insanity, but isn't it exactly such persons—fools, "weirdos," religious fanatics, the insane, "quacks," saints, and very ill people—who have historically been able to withdraw their allegiance to the Newtonian universe, often with no particular intention? Often such people don't know what they are doing, or why. In fact, persistence in such behavior is markedly dangerous to them, as in the case of Agnes Sampson, sent to the flames because she couldn't keep her mouth shut. In chapter 6 I suggested that Agnes may have tapped into the king's experience; perhaps she got a glimpse of the enormous world of connections, closed to us normal, hard-working folks by our matter-of-fact constructions, our climate of belief. Of course fools, saints, and poets have been telling us about this for centuries:

> How do you know but ev'ry Bird that cuts the airy way,
> Is an immense world of delight, closed by your senses five?[12]

"Realists"—sober, hard-headed folks—have always argued stoutly against accepting such tales as true, because they outrage "logic." But what if the logic of the universe is only something we bring to it? That is what quantum mechanics suggests.

"Time" itself is under question here. "The study of relativity," Zukav tells us, "can produce the remarkable experience that space and time are only mental constructions."[13] We have already noted that, according to quantum mechanics, "there is nothing but space-time and motion." A note from one of Zukav's physicist mentors adds that "the space-time continuum is not only curved, it also has topological properties, i.e., it can be connected in crazy ways, e.g., like a donut. It also can twist (i.e., torsion)."[14]

This suggests an explanation for one of the most remarkable accounts I know, that of William Seabrook's sudden (quantum?) leap forward in time. Actually, the leap in question was accomplished by Seabrook's girlfriend, whom he calls "Justine." She was what psychic researchers call a "sensitive." To assist her to achieve her visions, she and Seabrook practiced "dervish-dangling," a technique adapted from the Rufiah, a sect of dervishes whom Seabrook had visited in Tripoli.

> I shall tell here at the beginning, instead of saving it for a later climax, the result of what happened one night when the dervish dangling got out of hand, through my carelessness, and catapulted Justine through what seemed to be the "slit" in time to a seeming experience in precognition whose denouement came many months later in a place three thousand miles away.

Justine was on tiptoe that night. I had arranged everything with unusual care, because we'd begun early and had
a chance to let it run, if it ran, for seven or eight hours—
even longer. We hadn't got round to inventing the mask
yet, so I had turned out all the lights, as she preferred, had
drawn the velvet curtains of the big studio window, so that
the room was almost in complete darkness. A soft light, less
than the softest moonlight, came from the street outside
through the thinner curtains of a smaller window. We had
tried it on former occasions with one arm, as the Rufiah
do—passing one wrist through the loop of a soft, heavy
rope dangling from a ring in the ceiling and then revolving
until the rope tightens to give the right tension—but she
had found that it worked better and left her mind more free
when she was fastened up by both wrists and "stayed put."
This left her helpless as a modern Andromeda—too helpless, in fact, because she didn't like being fussed over, or
eased, or interfered with. So we had worked out an
arrangement with the telephone books. On that night, all
three of them—The Manhattan, the Brooklyn, and the
Classified—were solidly under her feet when it began, so
that as she stood with her wrists fastened above her head,
she was slightly on tiptoe, but with her toes firmly on the
phone books. If the rope sagged, as it sometimes did, or the
soft straps round her writs slipped a little, she could push
one or more of the books out from under, with her toes,
without my interference, to restore the tension.

Sometimes, in a long evening, nothing at all would happen, and we'd give up. On other evenings when she went
through the "door," she would sometimes tell what was
happening in that other world in time-space, beyond our
three-dimensional horizon . . . if there is any such other
world. Just as often she'd be silent the whole time, and tell
me about it only afterward, if at all. In the near-darkness, it
frequently took a lot of patient waiting. I've sometimes
gone out and left her alone for a whole evening. I might as
well have gone out during the early part of this evening, for
nothing happened until close on toward ten o'clock, and

then I heard her shuffling the phone books with her toes, pushing one of them out from under, as I imagined, to increase the tension a little.

Soon she began to talk . . . dreamily at first. She was through the "door," and was having a lovely time. She seldom went through that door into any horror or violence. She was not like Nastatia Filipovna [another of Seabrook's subjects]. In her trances, or whatever they were, she nearly always encountered things that were good and beautiful. If there is any such other world, beyond our normal ken, there's at least one moral-weighted aphorism true there as here. Wherever you go, you have to take yourself with you. It's only if you have the soul of a werewolf here that you will turn into a werewolf, or encounter werewolves, on the other side of the "door." The things Justine encountered, in addition to being beautiful, were also sometimes surprising and amusing. She had never been in Europe then, but she was wandering along a quai, overlooking a river, and behind the quai was an enormous castle or palace. There were crowds, streetcars, shops, motorcars, people on bicycles. I though it might be London, as she described with delight the things she was glimpsing. She was walking. She stopped to look at little boats that passed in the stream. I wanted to ask her what language the street signs were in, what language the people in the streets were speaking—but we'd learned that such interruptions often short-circuited the contact. As she talked on, describing, and exclaiming at the quaintness or beauty of the buildings, I got the impression that it wasn't London. I wondered if it might be Budapest, or possibly a part of old Florence. It was on a big river, and it was lovely as she described it. But I wasn't very excited about it. Whatever specific city it turned out to be, she could easily have seen it in newsreels, in photos in the *National Geographic,* or in any casual, forgotten magazine—or perhaps in some old book she'd seen as a little girl and long since forgotten with her conscious memory. That's why supposed "clairvoyance" of this or any other sort is difficult to prove or make stand up.

She turned into a side street, leading away from the quai and the river, attracted by the sound of music, and presently came to a carnival, with merry-go-rounds, confetti, clowns, ferris wheels, booths, tents. It wasn't exactly a carnival either. There was a menagerie, she said; there were animal cages, there was a dancing bear with a pointed hat on its head; there were clowns. It was like a circus, only the clowns and animal wagons weren't under the tents. It puzzled her, but she was enjoying it. She was seeing one of the big street fairs on the continent—perhaps the *Foire de Neuilly*. But what if she was? She could have seen it first (and consciously forgotten about it while it stuck in her subconscious) in a topical newsreel—or for that matter in a screen play made in Hollywood. She went into one of the tents presently to see the trained lions. There was a woman lion-tamer, on an elevated stage, behind bars, putting a lion through its tricks. Justine presently chuckled a little. It was a funny lion. It was an *old*, tired lion, and it looked as if it had been kept in moth balls. The lion-tamer was "cute" in her boots and red jacket. She was pretty. She was pretty, even if she did have blondined hair and too much red paint on her cheeks. Now she was going to put her head in the lion's mouth. Yes, she was lying down with the lion. Oo, yes she did! She'd put her head right inside the lion's enormous mouth. And afterward the lion had got up and yawned. It had come to the front of the cage and yawned. "If that was *my* lion," Justine giggled, "I'd teach it to *roar.*"

Justine was silent now, in the semidarkness, for a couple of minutes, and then let out a gasp and giggle, and said, "I don't believe it! It didn't happen!" I was wondering what she didn't believe, what didn't happen, when she burst into gales of laughter, and cried,

"Yes, it did happen! It really did happen! The others thought it was a joke at first, a part of the show. And I did too. But it really happened. That woman in the front row with the baby was simply too funny!"

Justine had presently left the street fair and was going back to her hotel, or wherever she was going in the trance, and had taken a taxi. She was still calm, apparently still enjoying herself. Her voice was calm, smooth, pleased. I had forgotten, almost as completely as she had, the other Justine who had been standing all that time with her wrists drawn up above her head, there on her tiptoes, on the phone books. And now in a period of silence, I didn't like the sound of that other Justine's breathing. And I switched on the light.

It was now nearly two o'clock in the morning, and the last shuffling of the phone books, or any other movement, had been before 10 P.M. What she had done had been to push or kick all three of the thick phone books aside. For more than four hours, she had dangled there clear of the floor, suspended by the wrists, her whole weight hanging by her wrists, with her toes swinging nearly two inches clear of the floor. The lips from which that always calm, tranquil, amused, and at times gay and laughing, talk had been streaming, were bitten and bruised by her own teeth, and her face was contorted as that of a girl who weeps when no tears flow. Her eyes were glassy, clear, ecstatic, wide open in the light. The light bewildered her, but she was still far away. When I lifted her and loosed the straps around her wrists, she said, "Don't! Don't! I'm seeing. . . ."

I carried her to a couch, made her drink a little brandy, and began chafing her wrists. We never quarreled—but that night she was so angry that she threatened never to come back.

I said, "Look at your wrists! They'll be black and blue tomorrow, and your thumbs will be numb for a week."

She said, "My thumbs! I thought you were so brave and daring, and you tell me my wrists will be black and blue! They're *my* wrists and my thumbs. Something wonderful was happening to me. It was different from anything that has ever happened before."

I said, "You played a dirty trick on me there in the dark. I wouldn't have done that to you—for four hours. And I wouldn't have let you do it to yourself. . . ."

She said, "You lost your nerve and I'm ashamed of you. I tell you this was different.

How different, how on the edge of something possibly tremendous if it could ever be controlled—how perhaps actually *over* the edge, Justine had been that night, I didn't know, and I still didn't know the following summer, when more than six months had passed, and she was on her first visit to Europe, and we were spending a week together in the south of France.

One afternoon we drove to Avignon, and were walking along the quai toward the old bridge, with the Papal Palace on the left, when she said:

"But this is it! This is where I was that night, the night we quarreled because you brought me back too soon. There's the man on the bicycle, with a derby hat, those three girls with shawls, that priest on a bicycle. I remember how funny the priest was, in robes, with a beard, on a bicycle. . . ."

I was a little bit scared, and still skeptical. I thought, "She can have seen Avignon without ever being in Europe before. The Papal Palace, the quai, the famous bridge, are travelogue stock subjects." And I thought of another point too, which I maliciously made.

"You never mentioned any priest on a bicycle, or a man with a derby hat on a bicycle either."

"Didn't I, Willie?" she asked. "I don't know what I said that night. Did I tell you about the street fair? Listen, you can almost hear the music now. The merry-go-round will be up that second corner, round another turn, with the tents and clowns."

We made the first turn, and I began to hear the merry-go-round, and it gave me goose flesh. The back of my neck felt cold. I was goose pimples all over, and we were holding each other's hands pretty tightly when we walked into that street fair. I tried to get a grip on myself, I kept thinking, "No, it can't be. There's a fair here every summer, same fair, same clowns, same animals, same dancing bear, same lion-tamer. She must have seen it in a film somewhere." I kept telling myself she must have seen it in a film somewhere, when we came to the lion-tamer's tent, and went in and sat down. I kept telling myself that the lion-tamer is always a little woman in boots, red jacket, with blondined hair, and too much rouge on her cheeks. It was always an elderly lion, and she always lay down and put her head in its mouth. But did it always yawn, as it was now doing? It must have yawned, in whatever film or travelogue Justine had seen and forgotten. For it was yawning now. It was surely a part of the act. Justine said, and I began to have goose pimples again, "If it was *my* lion, I'd teach it to roar."

Then as we sat there, she said, excitedly, "It's going to turn now! It's going to come to the front of the cage and turn its back! Yes, it's going to do it!"

"Do what?" I asked, and she whispered, *"It's going to wet those people down there in the front row."*

The front row benches were six feet away from the barred stage, and on a lower level. The great cat lumbered, sidling to the front bars, turned its back, half squatted, and loosed a mighty stream of amber liquid, that arced through the air and splashed on the clothes and faces of the people in the middle of the row down yonder.

The audience was amazed, then giggling, then shouting with joy, and Justine burst into gales of laughter. She clutched me and said, "Watch that woman with the baby! She's going to get up now. . . ."

The woman, a bareheaded peasant in a black shawl, holding aloft a wailing brat whose face she was wiping, arose, climbed on the bench, and screamed furiously in the Marseillais dialect:

"You saw it! I call you to witness! In the face! In the eyes of my darling innocent! In the face, it pissed! In the face of my little Pouponne! For this I paid two francs and fifty centimes!"

The audience howled and egged her on. I said to Justine, "Could you understand what she said?"

Justine said, "No, I couldn't understand a word of it,

either time. But it was simply too funny, wasn't it? I'm glad you've seen it too."

I was more disturbed, perhaps, than I have ever been about anything. I was thinking of the "slit" in time, of the Einstein corollaries, of a phrase written by Columbia University's greatest mathematician, Dr. Cassius Jackson Keyser, "Simultaneity of events is relative, not absolute; the sense of time is only an imperfect sense of a fourth dimension in space." Yet I was unconvinced. There's a tenet in philosophic logic known as "Occam's Razor." It says, *"Essentia non sunt multiplicanda praeter necessitatem."* I thought, "It *can* be that this whole thing has happened before. It can be part of the act . . . just as the yawning might be a part of the act . . . and it *can* have been caught in a film—or Justine can have read it."

Next morning I went and tried to shave the little lion-tamer with Occam's Razor. She thought I was a lawyer, or making a complaint, and said I'd better talk with her husband, who was the manager of the show. I convinced them that I was a journalist, and that all I wanted to know was whether the thing had been part of the act—or if not part of the act, whether by chance it had ever happened before.

"But mon dieu!" they protested, of course it had never happened before! They had only bought the old lion in January. They had bought it because it was an old "trouper" born in a cage, born in the show business.

Had they ever heard of such a thing happening before with *any* lion? They laughed. "Not through the bars of the cage! Not on the audience! It had been funny, if one hadn't been splashed. Impossible, unexpected things animals did were always the funniest. One night with those three performing bears at the Médrano . . . " the woman was saying, and I asked,

"Did you work at the Médrano?"

"All my life," she said proudly. *"This is the first season I have ever worked in a street fair."*[15]

Once again, we must consider our source. Seabrook is an entertaining author, and one who frequently experimented with "the supernatural." Has the entertainer here, or the believer, to put it most kindly, got the better of the reporter? Again, I think not. Anyone familiar with the body of Seabrook's work will know his book *Asylum,* in which he painfully confronts his alcoholism, or his autobiography, in which he often questions his own motives severely. Everything about the man speaks of honesty and faithful dealing. He was as perplexed by this event as any of his readers might be, and he never deluded himself that he could identify the principle involved. "Whatever fleeting power she [Justine] possessed," he concludes, "we could never control it to the slightest extent."[16]

Remember, according to quantum mechanics, or more specifically, Einstein's special theory of relativity, "space and time are not two separate things, but . . . together they form space-time."[17]

> The Newtonian view of space and time is a *dynamic* picture. Events *develop* with the passage of time. Time is one-dimensional and *moves* (forward). The past, present, and future happen in that order. The special theory of relativity, however, says that it is preferable, and more useful, to think in terms of a *static,* non-moving picture of space and time. This is the space-time continuum. In this static picture, the space-time continuum, events do not develop, they just are. If we could view our reality in a four-dimensional way, we would see that everything that now seems to unfold before us with the passing of time, already exists *in toto,* painted, as it were, on the fabric of space-time. We would see all, the past, the present, and the future with one glance.[18]

Then it may be possible for certain deranged mental states—I use the term "deranged" advisedly—to get a glimpse of the fabric of space-time. Quantum mechanics does not "prove" this, or demonstrate it—it merely says that it is possible.

Even more difficult to comprehend than space-time, perhaps, is the Many Worlds Theory. The underlying reasoning is complex, but the problem of measurement of the wave function—"The fundamental theoretical quantity in quantum mechanics is the wave function"[19]—led physicists Hugh Everett, John Wheeler, and Neil Graham to propose "an endlessly proliferating number of *different branches of reality!*"[20]

"The wave function" is difficult to grasp. One physicist calls it "the physicists' description of reality."[21] Zukav defines it as "a mathematical fiction that represents all the possibilities that can happen to an observed system when it interacts with an observing system (a measuring device)." As soon as "the observing system" identifies a *result*—the actual fulfillment of one of these possibilities—all the others cease to exist; this is called "the collapse of the wave function."[22] This seems logical enough, but the problem with it is in measurement—what happens to all the other possibilities? Orthodox quantum mechanics says that they vanish, but Mssrs. Everett, Wheeler and Graham solve this problem "in the simplest way possible." Their theory says that "the wave function is a real thing, all of the possibilities that it represents are real, and *they all happen*" (Zukav's emphasis). All the possibilities actualize, "but in different worlds that coexist with ours!"[23]

As far-fetched as this theory seems at first, it does solve immediately certain basic problems. Wave functions don't collapse, they just keep splitting as they develop. If you hesitate between eating an apple, and putting it down, you are setting up a table of possibilities, just as though you were engaged in an experiment. When you actually take up the apple and eat it, all the other possibilities inherent in the situation "collapse." But according to the Many Worlds Theory, the universe is immediately split, into the "reality" in which you eat the apple, and the many other possible realities, which include your leaving the apple in the dish, or dropping it, or throwing it out the window. Thus there are an infinite number of universes, all coexisting, but completely and definitively separated from each other. "The Many Worlds Interpretation of quantum mechanics says that different editions of us live in many worlds simultaneously, an uncountable number of them, and all of them are real." Zukav adds, "Quantum physics is stranger than science fiction."[24]

Just as strange, perhaps, as the many folktales, legends, or rumors of "other dimensions" which have been with humankind since the dawn of consciousness. Fortean writers—the name comes from Charles Fort, the doyen of a school of iconoclasts who enjoy reminding orthodoxy of its weaknesses—have kept many of these cases before our eyes. One of the earliest and most famous of these is that related by William of Newbridge, of the sudden appearance, during the reign of King Stephen (1135–1154), of a strange boy and girl near Bury St. Edmunds. They looked like any other children, except that their skin color had a slightly green tinge, and they spoke a language that no one could understand. There was great difficulty in finding food that they could, or would, eat. Even after this was accomplished, the boy, who seemed deeply depressed, languished and died. The girl gradually grew accustomed to the ways of Suffolk, lost her greenish hue, was baptized and eventually married. She was always, however, of a "loose and wanton disposition." The clothes these mysterious children were wearing, incidentally, were of "a material unknown to the people of the neighbourhood."[25]

The climate of belief of the period had no difficulty in identifying the children as "fairies," and their mysterious world as "fairyland." Our age would surely nominate them as "aliens," and mount a search for their starship. Earlier times saw the Virgin and the Saints; we see flying saucers. Once again, "reality" is defined by what we think.

These green children appeared to a notably credulous age; but what of the six persons who, between January 14, 1920, and December 9, 1923, were discovered wandering on the streets of, or near the small town of Romford, Essex, England, "unable to tell how they got there, or anything else about themselves"? What about the naked man who suddenly appeared on High Street, Chatham, Kent, on January 6, 1914? "The day was bitterly cold, yet the man ran about wildly without a stitch on him. People walking on the same street testified later that they had seen the man come from nowhere. He was just there, confused and frightened." Doctors declared him insane—and perhaps he was, by that time.[26]

We could adduce hundreds of such cases. No doubt 95 percent of them may be explained by "natural causes," and some have already been revealed as hoaxes; but what of the remaining 5 percent? In the past there has been much speculation as to "various planes of reality," "mirror-universes," and "slits in time and space." Are these theories stranger than the Many Worlds interpretation of quantum mechanics?

Some of these accounts are truly bizarre: my favorite is the story of Mr. and Mrs. Chapman, out hunting for flowers to decorate a charity event.

> While Mrs. Chapman went to examine a large flowering cherry tree, her husband stood looking at some primroses. When he looked up again, the apartment buildings were gone!
>
> He could see his wife in the distance and everything seemed perfectly normal, but the apartment buildings simply were not there!
>
> "Then something else happened," Chapman wrote. "Everything changed; a vast open nothingness surrounded me. But I had not lost my orientation because the sun was shining and gave me my bearings. But had I entered another dimension? And would I get out?"
>
> Chapman deduced that the "exit" must be his point of entry, so he crossed two sticks on the ground to mark his position. Then he began to walk toward where the apartment buildings should have been. He walked on and on. There were no apartment buildings, no roads, no traffic, ". . . just a vast open space and no sign of any kind of life."
>
> Lest his wife become worried about him, Chapman hastened back to where he had left the crossed sticks. He saw his wife near him and spoke to her.
>
> "How you startled me!" she exclaimed. "Where have you been? I called you and searched for you and couldn't find you."
>
> Now everything was back to normal, Chapman observed. The apartment buildings were where they should be. The shrubs, trees, and traffic were once again visible.
>
> "But I found one odd thing. The ground where I had been standing was soft and bare. I could see my footprints going toward the flats—but they suddenly ended as if I had

stepped off the ground into thin air! And my return path started in the same manner as the outgoing marks suddenly had vanished!"

Chapman concludes his report by musing: "But the question remains: had I stepped into the past, the future, or another space dimension?"[27]

We have not had the opportunity to have Mr. Chapman examined by psychiatrists, or tested by a lie detector. Whether his story is true or not, it takes its place in an enormous catalogue of such tales, for which the Many Worlds Theory, if it cannot offer proof, at least suggests a line of conjecture. One more aspect of quantum mechanics is particularly provocative in our area, and that is Bell's Theorem, which implies that, "at a deep and fundamental level, the 'separate parts' of the universe are connected in an intimate and immediate way."[28]

Bell's Theorem originated in an experiment with particles. In what physicists call a "two-particle system of zero spin," the spin of each of the particles in the system cancels the other. If one of the particles has an upward spin, then the other must have a downward spin. If one spins right, the other must spin left. No matter how these particles are oriented, their spins are always equal and opposite.

These particles may be separated in a way that does not affect their spin. One of them may then be directed through a magnetic field, which will change its spin, say from right to left. When that happens, the other particle automatically changes its spin, in the opposite direction. But how does the second particle "know" that it is to change its spin? It seems evident that what we do in one area affects events in another, perhaps widely separated (in particle terms), area, and immediately! This phenomenon is called the EPR effect, after its observers, Einstein, Podolsky, and Rosen.

The catch is that whatever is the agency of communication between these two particles, it is theoretically faster than the speed of light, long held by physicists to be an absolute. The phenomenon also seems to violate the principle of local causes, which states that "what happens in one area does not depend on variables subject to the controls of an experimenter in a distant space-like area."[29] Einstein thought that the EPR effect, therefore, since it violated both the principle of local causes and the absolute speed of light, proves that quantum mechanics is an incomplete theory—or else there is no real independence in things that are spatially separated from each other. That seemed to him totally unacceptable. But today physicists are seriously examining that possibility, which mystics and seers have always claimed as fact.

Bell's Theorem carries the argument forward. Working with polarized photons, he demonstrated that the principle of local causes, however reasonable it sounds, is "mathematically incompatible with the assumption that the statistical predictions of quantum theory are valid;" quite a finding, considering that *the statistical predictions of quantum mechanics are always correct.*"[30] In 1964, Bell's Theorem was still untested. By 1972, the Clauser-Freedman experiment gave it strong confirmation.

Now physics is entering "the supernatural" by the front door. Bell's Theorem seems clearly to provide a rationale for ESP, which often happens, or is reported to happen, instantly, in defiance of both the principle of local causes and the absolute speed of light. The implications are awesome. Among them is the suggestion that the old Magickal Universe of Correspondences—"as above, so below"—as articulated by Paracelsus and others, is actually closer to the truth than is the whole structure of classical physics; that "the mother who rose in alarm at the same instant that her daughter's distant automobile crashed into the tree"[31] (Zukav's example, p. 288) is neither a quack, nor a hysteric, nor a mischievous inventor of incredible tales. Think how many such stories deal with a mother's, or a sweetheart's, sudden intuition that a soldier, son, or lover, has been killed or wounded. There is obviously a connection between the two actors in these dramas which is independent of time and space as they are conventionally understood—but not necessarily as quantum mechanics understand them.

My great-grandfather Alden Hoyt had psychic powers. Typically they came upon him after a life-threatening illness. We have good evidence of the efficacy of these powers: he kept his children home the morning of the blizzard of 1888, for instance, when no one else suspected a storm. This was in South Dakota; some of the children who did go to school that day froze to death trying to get home. Had his illness somehow enabled him to get a look at the "fabric of space-time"?

The wildest story told of him concerns his automatic writing, at which he was proficient. On June 21, 1911, his daughter-in-law's father, Carlyle Goodrich, lay dying. He knew the man, of course, though not well, but he suddenly picked up an envelope lying at hand, and wrote on it, "You will hear that I died at 12^{15} today Carlyle Goodrich." This proved to be true, but more remarkable still, it was in Carlyle Goodrich's easily recognized handwriting! Alden Hoyt wrote a crabbed, arthritic hand, while Carlyle Goodrich wrote beautiful Spencerian, and it was in this style that the message was written.

As is not the case with most of these anecdotes, the key evidence—the envelope—survives. My Aunt Mary Perry, who now possesses it, has sent me a clear Xerox copy of it. I own Carlyle Goodrich's diaries and the handwriting on the envelope is the same as that in those diaries.

We are slowly assimilating bits of knowledge that indicate our relationship to an entity much greater than ourselves. In the process we have to painfully rid ourselves of some of our most cherished prejudices and oldest habits of thought, as David Finkelstein writes, in our never-ending quest for the unattainable. Some of the earliest fumblings toward this noble goal have been abhorred as witchcraft, and their perpetrators punished even unto death. Perhaps it is time now at last for us to lay aside violence and impartially investigate all phenomena. We may find that the quackeries and superstitions of the past can take their place with the findings of Newton and Einstein, as building blocks in the never-finished edifice of science.

Notes
Index

Notes

1. Introduction to Witchcraft

1. James H. Neal, *Jungle Magic* (New York, 1966), pp. 20-23.
2. See *On the Trail of the Poltergeist* (New York, 1958) and *The Haunted Mind* (New York, 1959).
3. *Saducismus Triumphatus*, 3rd ed., enl. (original publication 1683). The 1700 edition advertises "the enlarged Narrative of the Daemon of Tedworth, or of the Disturbances at Mr. Mompesson's House, caused by Witchcraft, and the villany of the Drummer." Pt. 2, p. 49.
4. One of these last, after having caused bad weather in upstate New York, recently came to earth in a backyard in Washington County. "It was a circular saw," my informant reports; "you could see the teeth in the photograph. The fellow said he saw it light" (George Paige, private communication to the author).
5. While this argument was suggested at least as long ago as the early nineteenth century, it did not gain headway until the 1920's.
6. We ought not to suppose that our ancestors did not have these doubts. In fact, in the years before the persecutions actually gathered headway, the so-called "Dark Ages," these doubts were often in the ascendancy. Thus we read in the authoritative *Canon Episcopi* (ca. 900) about "certain abandoned women, perverted by Satan, seduced by illusions." The inquisitors were hard put to subvert the pervasive influence of this document, which had passed into canon law in the twelfth century.

2. Satan

1. *The Marriage of Heaven and Hell.*
2. "Address to the Deil."
3. Preface, *Lyrical Ballads* (London, 1800).
4. "The Infernal Parliament," in *The Square Egg* (London, 1924).
5. One of the best explanations I know of this situation occurs in one of the lesser-known poems of Frost, *A Masque of Reason.*
6. In an earlier version of this story (2 Sam. 24), God alone provokes David. This conception apparently was not suited to a more sophisticated age; hence the appearance of an intermediary in David's punishment, a "Satan." Jeffrey Russell believes that the sufferings of the Babylonian Captivity were decisive in bringing Satan to the fore (*Witchcraft in the Middle Ages* [Ithaca,

N.Y., 1972], pp. 106-7).

7. Montague Summers, ed. and trans. (London, 1928), p. 1.

8. The anthropological position that "devil" derives from "div" = "God" and is therefore cognate to "divine," is not accepted at present, to the best of my knowledge. The *OED* gives the Greek origin, as above. Margaret Murray apparently first put forth the suggestion; see Felix Morrow's Introduction to Montague Summers's *History of Witchcraft and Demonology*, 2d ed. (New York, 1956).

9. Monsignor F. M. Catharinet, "Demoniacs in the Gospel," in *Satan*, ed. Pere Bruno de Jesus-Marie, O.C.D. (New York, 1952), p. 170.

10. Rossell Hope Robbins, *Encyclopedia of Witchcraft and Demonology* (New York, 1959), p. 131.

11. *Death's Jest-Book*, 3:iii, 44-45.

12. *A Dictionary of Angels: Including the Fallen Angels* (New York, 1967), p. 190.

13. Ibid., p. 57.

14. Henry Charles Lea, *Materials Toward a History of Witchcraft*, 3 vols., arr. and ed. Arthur C. Howland (New York, 1957), 1:28.

15. *A Dictionary of Angels*, p. 57.

16. Robbins, *Encyclopedia*, p. 132.

17. A. V. W. Jackson, quoted by I. J. S. Taraporewala, "Manichaeism," in *Ancient Religions*, ed. Vergilius Ferm (New York, 1950), p. 223.

18. Taraporewala, *Ancient Religions*, p. 221.

19. Susy Smith, *Today's Witches* (Englewood Cliffs, N.J., 1970), p. 103.

20. *Adventures in Arabia* (New York, 1927).

21. Information and quotes taken from Louis Massignon, "The Yezidis of Mount Sindjar," in *Satan*, ed. Pere Bruno de Jesus-Marie, O.C.D. (New York, 1952), pp. 158-59.

22. *Adventures in Arabia*, pp. 308-9.

23. Ibid., p. 309.

24. Ibid., pp. 325-26.

25. Quoted by Margaret A. Murray, *The Witch-Cult in Western Europe* (London, 1967, paperback), p. 25. Quotation translated by Hoyt.

3. Origins

1. Reginald Scot, *The Discoverie of Witchcraft* (Carbondale, Ill., 1964), 6. 1. 109-10.

2. While it is a pity to qualify this striking phrase, some elucidation of it seems necessary: had Samuel become a god after his death? The *Interpreter's Dictionary of the Bible* has this helpful note: "The word *ilu*, 'God,' is used in Akkadian in reference to the spirits of the departed." *Interpreter's Dictionary of the Bible*, 4 vols., ed. George A. Buttrick (New York, 1962), 2:237.

3. Henry Charles Lea, *Materials Toward a History of Witchcraft*, 3 vols., arr.

and ed. Arthur C. Howland (New York, 1957), 1: 121.

4. Ibid., p. 92.

5. Rossell Hope Robbins, *Encyclopedia of Witchcraft and Demonology* (New York, 1959), p. 28.

6. Howland, Lea's *Materials*, 1:157.

7. *The New Catholic Encyclopedia* (New York, 1967), 14: 111.

8. Aquinas's role in witchcraft is still being debated. Some recent scholarship tends to absolve him: Norman Cohn, for example, says Aquinas "has no place for anything remotely resembling witches" *(Europe's Inner Demons* [New York, 1975] p. 174); and Jeffrey Russell points out that Aquinas's views "in no way approached the witchcraft found in popular writings" *(Witchcraft in the Middle Ages* [Ithaca, N.Y., 1972] p. 147). On the other hand, H. R. Trevor-Roper calls Aquinas "after Augustine . . . the second founder of demonological science" *(Religion, the Reformation and Social Change* [London, 1967] p. 96). The most thorough study of this question, Charles E. Hopkin's "The Share of Thomas Aquinas in the Growth of the Witchcraft Delusion" (Ph.D. diss., University of Pennsylvania, 1940), arrives at this measured conclusion: "While the witchcraft literature dressed the pact with Satan in a variety of circumstantial details drawn from witch trials, and formalized it into a contract, nevertheless the informal 'Tacit or expressed pact,' a mere association with demons, as found in Thomas and Augustine was the essential nucleus" (p. 174).

9. Robert Graves, *The Greek Myths*, 2 vols. (Baltimore, 1955), 1:17.

10. The Jews too, presumably, would have gone through a shift to the patriarchal system so evident in the Old Testament. This has not escaped commentary by scholars; Graves, for example, cites David's formation of a royal harem as an instance of the solidifying of patriarchal power (Graves, p. 20). One might go back considerably before that, to Adam and Eve, for evidence of mythic apologia for female subordination. One thing seems clear: that patriarchal rule was both earlier and more thorough in Israel than in Greece.

11. Quoted by Montague Summers, *Geography of Witchcraft* (New York, 1958), p. 7.

12. Ibid., pp. 7-8.

13. Introduction to his translation of Hesiod's *Theogony* (New York, 1953), p. 31.

14. Hesiod's *Theogony*, pp. 64-65.

15. Ibid., p. 65.

16. Brown, Introduction, Hesiod's *Theogony*, p. 18.

17. Homer, *Odyssey* 10.

18. *The Greek Myths*, 2:367.

19. N. O. Brown, *Hermes the Thief*, (1947; reprinted ed., New York, 1969).

20. Appolonius Rhodius, *Argonautica*, 3 vols., trans. Edward P. Coleridge (New York, 1960), 3:171.

21. Ibid., p. 195.

22. The witches of Thessaly were notorious throughout the ancient world.
23. Ebb tide, when souls depart this life.
24. Ovid's *Metamorphoses*, trans. Frank Justus Miller (London, 1946), 1. 7. 361-63.
25. *The Greek Myths*, 1:335.
26. Ibid., 92-93.
27. Ibid., p. 93.
28. *Histories* 2. 51, trans. Harry Carter (New York, 1958), 1:113.
29. *The Greek Myths*, 1:102.
30. *The Ordeal of Richard Feverel*, ch. 1.
31. *The Greek Myths*, 2:255-56.
32. A much shorter version of his theory is available in an essay called "The Personal Muse," in *Oxford Addresses on Poetry* (New York, 1962).
33. The Sixth Satire, Dryden translation, lines 429-35.
34. F. Guirand and A. V. Pierre, "Roman Mythology," in *Larousse Encyclopedia of Mythology* (New York, 1959) p. 223.
35. Ibid.
36. *Geography of Witchcraft*, p. 35.
37. *The Golden Ass*, trans. Robert Graves (New York, 1953), p. 39.
38. *Satyricon*, trans. Jack Lindsay (New York, 1932), pp. 45-47.
39. Reprinted in Rossell Hope Robbin's *Encyclopedia of Witchcraft and Demonology*, pp. 75-77. This quotation p. 76.

4. The Development of the Orthodox Position

1. Some of these are now understood to be based on forged documents. See ch. 5 of this study.
2. *Encyclopedia of Witchcraft and Demonology* (New York, 1959), p 549.
3. Ibid., p. 549.
4. Introduction, *The God of the Witches* (London, 1970, paperback), pp. 21-22.
5. For other objections to these theories, see Jeffrey Russell: ". . . The argument that the Inquisition invented witchcraft because it had run out of heretics to prosecute cannot be accepted. In reality, heresy had never been so widespread as it was in the fourteenth and fifteenth centuries" (*Witchcraft in the Middle Ages* [Ithaca, N.Y., 1972], pp. 39-40).
6. "It was the Calvinist revolution which brought the first witch-law to Scotland in 1563 and thus inaugurated a century of terror." H. R. Trevor-Roper, *Religion, the Reformation and Social Change* (London, 1967), p. 138.
7. Montague Summers, *The History of Witchcraft and Demonology*, 2d ed. (New York, 1956), p. 13.
8. Ibid., p. 13.
9. Ibid., p. 65.
10. Robbins, *Encyclopedia*, p. 287.
11. Ibid.

12. Henry Charles Lea, *Materials Toward a History of Witchcraft*, 3 vols., arr. and ed. Arthur C. Howland (New York, 1957), 1:220-22.
13. *Geography of Witchcraft (New York*, 1958), p. 377.
14. Lea, *Materials*, 1:22L.
15. Ibid. p. 202.
16. Bull of Gregory IX, 13 June 1233, in Lea *Materials*.
17. It is true that one of the greatest pre-witchcraft persecutions, that of the Knights Templars, was probably founded largely upon greed. The order had grown vastly rich, and Philip the Fair needed money. It is also noteworthy however that the Templars' religious reforms were causing great uneasiness in Church circles. Summers groups the charges against the Templars under five heads: defiling the cross (and with this is coupled the *osculum infame*, kiss of shame, another universal charge at the later witch trials; witches, like Templars, were supposed to be obligated to kiss the devil's posterior), idolatry, altering the Holy Mass, granting of absolution by laymen, and the practice of sodomy *(Geography of Witchcraft*, p. 370).
18. *Geography of Witchcraft*, p. 53L.
19. Ibid., p. 533.
20. This body was the spawn of "heresy and ecclesiastical efficiency," as Jeffrey Russell puts it (p. 154). At first, heresy was left to the local authorities, the bishops; but the question grew too important to be left in their hands: "Gregory IX (1227-41), terrified of heresy, step by step initiated the procedures that created the centrally directed Inquisition." It became "a centralized institution staffed by Dominicans and, to a lesser extent, by Franciscans, and directed from Rome" (Russell, *Witchcraft in the Middle Ages*, p. 155).
21. Sometimes "Henricus" or "Heinrich" Kramer; "Jacobus" or "Jacob" Sprenger, according to one's usage. They were Germans; the bull was written in Latin; I am writing in English. The 1951 *Malleus* uses the English terms, as above. Kramer is sometimes referred to as "Henricus Institoris" ("institor" = "huckster").
22. *The Witch-Cult in Western Europe* (London, 1967, paperback), p. 169.
23. Sir Walter Scott, *Letters on Demonology and Witchcraft*, 4th ed. London, 1898), p. 169.
24. Introduction to *Malleus Maleficarum* (London, 1951).
25. *Malleus Maleficarum* 1. vi. 44.
26. Ibid. 1. vi. 47.
27. Ibid. 2. viii. 121.
28. Ibid. 2. vii. 150.
29. Ibid., Introduction, xiv.
30. Ibid. 3. xxx. 258-59.

5. The Triumph of Orthodoxy

1. *Los Caprichos* 43.
2. Norman Cohn, *Europe's Inner Demons: An Inquiry Inspired by the Great Witch-Hunt* (New York, 1975), p. 126.
3. Richard Kieckhefer, *European Witch Trials* (Berkeley, 1976), p. 17.
4. Rossell Hope Robbins, *Encyclopedia of Witchcraft and Demonology* (New York, 1959), p. 7.
5. *European Witch Trials*, p. 8.
6. Jeffrey Russell, *Witchcraft in the Middle Ages* (Ithaca, N.Y. 1972), p. 71.
7. Robbins, *Encyclopedia*, p. 455.
8. Lea thinks it "likely that there may have been an earlier edition" (*Materials Toward a History of Witchcraft*, 3 vols. arr. and ed. Arthur C. Howland [New York, 1957), 1:395).
9. Robbins, *Encyclopedia*, p. 236.
10. Ibid.
11. George Lyman Kittredge, *Witchcraft in Old and New England* 1929; reprint ed. (New York, 1958), p. 141.
12. Montague Summers, *History of Witchcraft and Demonology*, 2d, ed. (New York, 1956), p. 1.
13. By the time of *The Geography of Witchcraft*, published a year after the *History* (1927 and 1926 respectively), Summers has identified "an anti-Catholic temper" in the political writings of Bodin, whom he calls "a man of shifty and ever-shifting ideas" (p. 401).
14. Pennethorne Hughes, *Witchcraft* (London, 1952), p. 168.
15. Robbins, *Encyclopedia*, pp. 55, 54.
16. Hughes, *Witchcraft*, p. 186.
17. Charles Williams, *Witchcraft*, (New York, 1959), p. 256.
18. Robbins, *Encyclopedia*, p. 121.
19. Ibid., p. 56.
20. *Geography of Witchcraft*, p. 406.
21. A much-abbreviated title, published according to Summers in 1610 (and that a second edition). Robbins gives 1612 as the date, and Lea, 1613. These disparities may be explicable in terms of various editions, the details of which, concerning old authors, are often obscure.
22. *Geography of Witchcraft*, p. 407.
23. *Witchcraft in Old and New England.*
24. ". . . his researches did not prevent his being easily duped" (Wallace Notestein, *A History of Witchcraft in England from 1558 to 1718*, [1911; reprint ed. New York, 1968, paperback], p. 239).
25. Robbins, *Encyclopedia*, p. 224.
26. *Geography of Witchcraft*, p. 571.
27. Robbins, *Encyclopedia*, p. 355.
28. Ibid., p. 79.
29. *Materials Toward a History of Witchcraft*, 1:377, citing Hansen.

30. Robbins, *Encyclopedia*, p. 539.
31. *Witchcraft in Old and New England*, p. 340.
32. Ibid., p. 339.
33. Contrary to popular opinion, however, James did have a distinctly skeptical turn of mind. As his reign proceeded, he delighted in unmasking fraudulent witch-witnesses. Judged by the number of executions for witchcraft, his reign comes out very well.
34. Robbins, *Encyclopedia*, p. 309.
35. Quoted by Lea, *Materials Toward a History of Witchcraft*, 2:697.
36. Robbins, *Encyclopedia*, p. 480.
37. Note to Lea, *Materials Toward a History of Witchcraft*, 2:726-27.
38. There was considerable upset over Spee among the Jesuits, some of whom tried to get his book put on the Index.
39. *Witchcraft in Old and New England*, p. 360.
40. Ibid., p. 353.
41. This material was taken from Kittridge, *Witchcraft in Old and New England*, p. 355.
42. Quoted by Robbins, *Encyclopedia*, p. 201.
43. Thus Robbins *(Encyclopedia)*, p. 530, and Hole *(Witchcraft in England)*, p. 40. Hughes *(Witchcraft)* gives the terminal date as 1718, p. 174.
44. Robbins, *Encyclopedia*, p. 20.
45. She cites Valentine Penrose, *Erzsibet Bathory, La Comtesse Sanglante* (Paris, 1962) in her *Vampire* (London, 1965), p. 118. Seabrook's information, drawn from a man who had access to official records, seems better.
46. Robbins, *Encyclopedia*, p. 148.

6. The Anthropological Position

1. The theory that witchcraft was a surviving pagan religion had been advanced as early as the 1820's, but, until Margaret Murray, without attracting serious consideration.
2. A more plausible derivation, offered by Jeffrey Russell *(Witchcraft in the Middle Ages* [Ithaca, N.Y., 1972], p. 61), is from the Jewish sabbath. The twelfth synod of Toledo, in 681, voted approval of laws against "Jews and Magicians."
3. Charles Williams, *Witchcraft* (New York, 1959), pp. 121-22.
4. Edited by Thomas Davidson (Edinburgh, 1949).
5. Ibid., p. 147.
6. Wallace Notestein, *History of Witchcraft in England from 1558 to 1718* (Washington, 1911). I am using the Apollo edition of 1968, p. 95.
7. *Witchcraft in England*, (1945; reprint ed. London, 1966), p. 88.
8. Hughes, *Witchcraft* (London, 1952), pp. 179-80.
9. *Newes from Scotland*. In *Rowan Tree and Red Thread*, edited by Thomas Davidson, p. 152.

10. So my information (*Cambridge Bibliography of English Literature*, 1:624). Notestein says Shadwell (p. 121). With each new generation, scholarship revises its notions of the authorship of certain disputed sixteenth and seventeenth-century plays. Cf. attributions to "Beaumont and Fletcher."
11. *Witchcraft in England*, p. 90.
12. Quoted in Rossell Hope Robbins, *Encyclopedia of Witchcraft and Demonology* (New York, 1959), p. 296.
13. Robbins: "The Lancashire witches of 1612 are to be distinguished from the infamous swindle in 1634 at Pendle" (*Encyclopedia*, p. 298). Notestein: "The Lancashire witches of 1633 were the direct outcome of the Lancashire witches of 1612" (*History of Witchcraft in England*, p. 146).
14. Robbins, *Encyclopedia*, p. 232.
15. *Witch-Cult in Western Europe* (London, 1967, paperback), p. 72.
16. Robbins, *Encyclopedia*, pp. 307-8.
17. So also Burr and Robbins; my copy (1952) says "first published in MCMXXXI."
18. Julian Franklyn, *Death by Enchantment* (New York, 1971), p. 97.
19. Introduction to Henry Charles Lea, *Materials Toward a History of Witchcraft*, 3 vols. (1939; reprint ed. New York, 1957), p xxxviii.
20. Elliot Rose, *A Razor for a Goat: A Discussion of Certain Problems in the History of Witchcraft and Diabolism* (Toronto, 1962).
21. Elsewhere Russell seems to support the existence of a witchcraft cult: in speaking of material adduced by Carlo Ginzburg, he says, "no firmer bit of evidence has ever been presented that witchcraft existed" (p. 42). Cohn, however, says that this opinion rests on Russell's misreading of the material.

7. The Psychological School

1. Prierias mentions this in 1521. See Rossell Hope Robbins, *Encyclopedia of Witchcraft and Demonology* (New York, 1959), pp. 257-58.
2. See for example John Nevius, *Demon Possession and Allied Themes* (Chicago, 1894), which is a detailed account of phenomena encountered by Nevius in the course of his lifelong missionary service in China.
3. Robert Burns, "Address to the Deil."
4. I might add that I once found one of these mystic knots in my own mailbox, while on the faculty of a large midwestern university. Knowing, fortunately, who my tormentor was likely to be, I found occasion to get the charm into her own husband's possession, so that when she came around later to tease me, I was able to send her packing in some confusion.
5. I am using the volume of selections from the *Essays*, the *Diary*, and lesser material translated and grouped together by Marvin Lowenthal as *The Autobiography of Michel de Montaigne* (London, 1935). This citation page 223.

6. Ibid., p. 221.
7. Ibid., pp. 92-94.
8. Robbins, *Encyclopedia*, p. 193.
9. This fear is the subject of folktales from many cultures; Ornella Volta, for example, notes that "it is with the vagina that the Eskimo vampire devours her victims" (*The Vampire* [London, 1965], pp. 49-50). She quotes an observation of Freud to Marie Bonaparte, that the fear of the vagina originates in the castration complex (p. 49). Some indications of the extent of this anxiety among the aboriginal Indo-Europeans may be gathered from N. M. Penzer's privately printed *Poison Damsels* (London, 1952). One is most likely, however, to encounter the subject in bawdry; there is a standard, much elaborated "dirty joke" constructed on it. I recall seeing a cartoon on the subject within the last few years in the *East Village Other*.
10. Quoted by Robbins, *Encyclopedia*, p. 57.
11. "Would God that the Roman people had but one neck!" "Life of Caligula," ch. 30.
12. de Nion, quoted by Aldous Huxley, *The Devils of Loudun* (New York, 1952), p. 220.
13. Ibid.
14. Ibid., p. 216.
15. Ibid., p. 262.
16. Robbins, *Encyclopedia*, pp. 195-96.
17. Ibid., p. 537.
18. Montague Summers, *Geography of Witchcraft* (New York, 1958), p. 235.
19. Christina Hole, *Witchcraft in England* (1945; reprint ed. London, 1966), p. 59.
20. Lea, *Materials Toward a History of Witchcraft*, 3 vols. (New York, 1957), 3:1328.
21. Charles Williams, *Witchcraft* (New York, 1959) p. 298.
22. *The Reach of the Mind* (New York, 1968), p. 204.
23. Nandor Fodor, *The Haunted Mind* (New York, 1959), p. 10.
24. *The Devils of Loudun*, p. 223.

8. The Pharmacological School

1. *Formicarius* (Helmstadt, 1692), 2:iv, 200-202. This incident may be found in Henry Charles Lea, *Materials Toward a History of Witchcraft*, 3 vols. (New York, 1957), 1:260-61, and Robbins, *Encyclopedia of Witchcraft and Demonology* (New York, 1959), p. 364, among other source books.
2. *De Miraculis Rerum Naturalium* (Antwerp, 1560), 2:xxvi. I am using Lea's account (*Materials*, 2:913).
3. *Tractatus* 30. 121-24. Grillandus, it may be recalled from ch. 5, is also well represented in the sourcebooks.
4. *Hexenprozess und Geistesstörung* (Munich, 1891), pp. 68-77. Quoted by Lea, *Materials*, 2:914.

5. "The Witches' Pharmacopeia," *Bulletin of The Johns Hopkins Hospital* 7 (August 1896):65. Many scholars have been puzzled by the frequent occurrence in old recipes of parsley, which, Fletcher reminds us, had important significance both of death and regeneration for ancient peoples.

6. "Flying Ointments," app. 5 to Margaret A. Murray's *Witch-Cult in Western Europe* (London, 1921). In the paperback edition (London, 1967), the appendix occupies pp. 279-80.

7. John Charde, M.D., Sharon Clinic, Sharon, Conn. Dr. Charde also suggests that the brains of certain animals, often listed as ingredients, may contain elements capable of inducing imbalances of perception: "serotonin and hystamine-like substances." (Private correspondence.)

8. Clark, in *Murray's Witch-Cult in Western Europe*, p. 280.

9. Appendix to Montague Summers, *The Werewolf* (London, 1933), pp. 291-92.

10. *De La Lycanthropie, Transformation, et Extase des Sorciers* (Paris, 1615).

11. What with the advances both in language and in botany since de Nynauld's day, determining the precise meaning of some of his ingredients is troublesome. I have translated those I think significant; but the reader will surely want to know about "synochytides, which makes you see the shades of hell, that is, evil spirits," or its benign counterpart, which "makes the images of holy angels appear." As far as I can determine, we are dealing here in *lithomancy*, the art of divining or conjuring by precious stones. *Synochytides* appears to be drawn from "synochitis" "a kind of precious stone now unknown," according to Pliny. This supposition gains strength from the resemblance of anachitides to "anachites" = "anancites," "a name of the diamond as a remedy for sadness and trouble of mind" (*Harper's Latin Dictionary*, 1907).

As for "pentaphilon," that is cinquefoil, an apparently harmless five-leaved plant; "L'acorum" is another kind of rush or sweet flag; and the "feuilles" are poplar leaves. The two hard ones are "cyguë" and "l'hyuroye." My present tack on cyguë is that it may be the swan flower (cygne = -swan); "l'hyuroye" may be an early form of "Hyereois," from Hyères, some plant or other specific from that locality. Obviously there is room for more research in this area, but some of these questions, like that of "persil," will probably never be fully resolved.

12. *The Werewolf*, pp. 98-99, for both de Nynauld's and Summers's remarks.

13. *American Journal of Pharmacy* 130 (May 1958): 171-74.

14. Ibid., p. 173, n. 7.

15. Ibid., p. 174.

16. Ibid. At the time of his death, Professor Conklin was at work on certain effects of *bufotenine* (*bufo*, a toad; toads were associated with witches, who were often accused of poisoning people by toad venom.).

17. *The Pains of Opium*, explanatory note, and entry for May 1818. Remember, de Nynauld gives opium as an ingredient in witches' ointments.

18. *Les Paradis Artificiels*, in *Oeuvres Complètes*, ed. Jacques Crépet (Paris, 1928), p. 61.

19. *Le Club des Hachichins,* in *Oeuvres Complètes* (Genève: Slatkine Reprints, 1978), 4:441, 450.
20. In *Oxford Addresses on Poetry* (New York, 1962).
21. Ibid., pp. 134, 135.
22. *Jivaro* (London, 1953), p. 74.
23. Ibid., p. 115.
24. Alkaloids very commonly have this effect; it is known to those who have had their pupils enlarged with belladonna for the purpose of eye examinations. Graves observed that all the shades had to be drawn for his *psilocybe* experiments: "the least light, even strained through the eyelids, becomes painful as soon as the drug takes effect" *(Oxford Addresses on Poetry,* p. 134).
25. *Jivaro,* p. 127.
26. The full term is *Banisteriopsis Caapi.* Harner says *Caapi* refers to the drink brewed from the vine *(Natural History* [June-July 1968], p. 28).
27. *At Play in the Fields of the Lord* (New York, 1965), pp. 92, 93.
28. This was a feature of the Salem scare, which, incidentally, Harner takes seriously, on the basis of close study, as the result of a genuine outcropping of the cult. (Private correspondence.)
29. *Natural History,* pp. 28-29. This article, with other useful material, is reprinted in Harner's compilation *Hallucinogens and Shamanism* (New York, 1973).
30. My edition is paperback (New York: Ballantine Books, 1969). The material was apparently issued first by University of California Press in 1968, having served as Castaneda's doctoral thesis at UCLA.

9. Salem

1. *Witchcraft in Old and New England* (1929; reprint ed. New York, 1958).
2. In addition, recent research, which will be considered at some length later in this chapter, has identified Salem as the veritable epitome of economic and social changes which were beginning to occur among God's own people all over New England: new mercantile wealth and its accompanying social manifestations, developing in Salem *town,* colliding with the old communal Puritan ways, as fiercely maintained in conservative rural areas such as Salem *village* (now Danvers), the scene of the witch-persecutions. In short, the Puritan was becoming the Yankee, a process which could be painful.
3. Still the most complete account of these events is Charles Wentworth Upham's *Salem Witchcraft* (Boston, 1867), now again in print (Williamstown, Mass.: Corner House Publishers, 1971).
4. *Witchcraft at Salem* (New York, 1969), p. 32.
5. Rossell Hope Robbins, *Encyclopedia of Witchcraft and Demonology* (New York, 1959), p. 432.
6. Jurors' confessions of Error, January 14, 1696, reproduced in Calef's *More*

Wonders of the Invisible World (1700), and reprinted in full in Robbins, *Encyclopedia*, p. 448.

7. Thus Hansen, *Witchcraft at Salem*, p. 65. The phrasing is somewhat different in Mather, who has "poppets" for example, and "the Points being Outward" (*The Wonders of the Invisible World* [London, 1862], p. 137). Hansen is presumably using Woodward's collection of source documents, *Records of Salem Witchcraft* (Roxbury, Mass., 1864), although he also cites Mather in this section.

8. Mather, *Wonders of the Invisible World*, p. 130.

9. Ibid., p. 133.

10. "Cotton in his race for glory ran amuck. He was a man of 'overweening vanity,' panting for fame, and the strenuous mover in the trials" (M. V. Perley, *A Short History of the Salem Village Witchcraft Trials* [Boston, 1911], p. 22). John Greenleaf Whittier calls Mather a liar ("Calef in Boston"). In J. W. De Forest's *Witching Times*, originally published in *Putnam's Monthly Magazine* (Dec. 1856-Sept. 1857), he is compared to Titus Oates.

11. Hansen, *Witchcraft at Salem*, p. 193.

12. Mather, *Wonders of the Invisible World*, p. 148.

13. *The Devil in Massachusetts* (Garden City, N.Y.: Anchor Books, 1969), p. 171.

14. Kittredge, *Witchcraft in Old and New England*, p. 367.

15. *Salem Possessed / The Social Origins of Witchcraft* (Cambridge, Mass., 1974), and *Salem Village Witchcraft: A Documentary Record* (Belmont, Calif., 1972).

16. *Salem Possessed*, p. 213.

17. Ibid., p. 188.

18. Ibid., p. 215.

10. Occultists and Transcendentalists

1. *Witchcraft Today* (New York, 1955), p. 149.

2. Julian Franklyn, *Death by Enchantment* (New York, 1971), pp. 208-9.

3. *History of My Life*, trans. Willard R. Trask (New York, 1969), 7:28.

4. *Death by Enchantment*, p. 209.

5. *The Confessions of Aleister Crowley*, ed. John Symonds and Kenneth Grant (New York, 1970).

6. "The Wickedest Man in the World?" *Louisville-Courier Journal & Times*, 22 February 1970, p. F5.

7. He always insisted on this spelling.

8. *Confessions*, p. 424.

9. Ibid, p. 71.

10. *Witchcraft, Its Power in the World Today* (New York, 1940), p. 232.

11. Ed Sanders, "Charlie and the Devil," *Esquire* 66 (5 November 1971).

12. We may still speak of the occult, however, as one of *the ways to approach witchcraft*. A student of the occult like Elliot O'Donnell, who as far as I know does not profess himself a witch, has his own explanation of supernatural

phenomena. "My own view is that so complex a creature as man—complex both physically and psychologically—may have a representative spirit for each of his personalities. Hence on man's physical dissolution there may emanate from him a host of phantasms, each with a shape most fitting the personality it represents" (*Werwolves* [New York, 1965], p. 19). He goes on to suggest that what have been identified as werewolves may have been "in some instances," "phantasms of the dead, or Elementals." For a compelling exposition of this point of view in fiction, the student should consult Algernon Blackwood's short stories, particularly those collected in the volume entitled *John Silence* (London, 1908).

13. *A Book of Witchcraft* (New York, 1971), pp. 102-3.
14. *Witchcraft in the World Today*, p. 145.
15. I cannot refrain from giving Franklyn's comment on this report: "it is good to know that we were saved again by a party of prancing nudists, some of whom evidently caught cold and died, and that the navy and air force had nothing whatever to do with it" (p. 208).
16. Photograph caption opposite p. 81.
17. New York: Doubleday, 1969.
18. *The Truth About Witchcraft*, p. vii.
19. *Witchcraft from the Inside* (St. Paul, Minn., 1971), pp. 81-82.
20. *Witchcraft in the World Today*, p. 145.
21. New York: Coward-McCann, 1971.
22. *Mastering Witchcraft* (New York, 1970); *The Devil's Picturebook* (New York, 1971).
23. Reading, Mass., 1970.
24. *Brief Lives*, ed. Oliver Lawson Dick (Ann Arbor, Mich., 1962), p. 297.

11. Second Thoughts

1. Umbanda is one form of spiritism; there are others, such as candomblé.
2. Newton himself said, "That one body may act upon another at a distance through a vacuum without the mediation of anything else, by and through which their action and force may be conveyed from one to another, is to me so great an absurdity that, I believe, no man who has in philosophic matters a competent faculty of thinking could ever fall into it." *Procedings of the Royal Society*, quoted by Gary Zukav, *The Dancing Wu Li Masters: An Overview of the New Physics* (Bantam Books, 1980), p. 23.
3. David Finkelstein, foreword to Zukav, xxi.
4. Zukav, p. 112. Zukav's emphasis.
5. Zukav, p. 96.
6. Zukav, p. 37.
7. Zukav, p. 179.
8. Zukav, p. 78.

9. Alec Guinness, *Blessings in Disguise* (New York: Warner Books, 1987), pp. 34–35.

10. Zukav, p. 289.

11. Zukav, p. 172.

12. These lines are from William Blake *(The Marriage of Heaven and Hell)*, poet and madman, according to his contemporaries.

13. Zukav, p. 16.

14. Zukav, p. 179.

15. William Seabrook, *Witchcraft* (New York: Harcourt, Brace and Company, 1940), pp. 260–69.

16. Seabrook, p. 270.

17. Zukav, p. 121.

18. Zukav, p. 150.

19. Zukav, p. 80.

20. Zukav, p. 83.

21. Zukav, p. 80.

22. Zukav, p. 75.

23. Zukav, p. 83.

24. Zukav, p. 87.

25. From Lewis Spence, *The Fairy Tradition in Britain* (London: Rider and Company, 1984), p. 14.

26. Eric Norman, *Weird Unsolved Mysteries* (New York: Award Books, 1969), pp. 17, 16. The first case he abstracts from Charles Fort's *Lo*.

27. Norman took this account from the May 1967 issue of *Fate* magazine. Norman, p. 90.

28. Zukav, p. 282.

29. Zukav, p. 293.

30. Zukav, pp. 293, 290.

31. My wife has called my attention to a remarkable instance of this phenomenon among other members of our primate family. Dian Fossey tells how a mother gorilla acted suddenly to save her infant, who had become entangled in branches and was strangling to death. "An amazing aspect of the incident," Ms. Fossey writes, "was that Effie [the mother], whose back was turned towards her infant, was aware of Poppy's silent plight even before the human onlooker, facing both animals, realized anything was amiss." *Gorillas in the Mist* (Boston: Houghton Mifflin Company, 1983), p. 89.

Index